PRAISE FOR *FAIRVIEW*

"*Fairview* travels toward the unresolvable, morphing from neatly structured, stereotypical familiarity into rampant chaos and then into fractured, inquisitive aftermath. It begins by giving us something we think we've seen before, then estranges us from it and from ourselves as viewers of it, then cracks the whole thing open entirely and forces everyone in the room, actors and audience, to reckon with the broken pieces . . . With the world that we've built and the racism we've poured into its foundations, will any of us, Drury asks, ever be able to look around us at a view that is, in the truest sense, fair?"

—SARA HOLDREN, *NEW YORK/VULTURE*

"*Fairview* argues for the possibility of people of color representing themselves, onstage and off, without an overlay of white perception, judgment and narrative. It gently body-checks privilege."

—ADAM FELDMAN, *TIME OUT NEW YORK*

"It is rare these days to encounter a dramatic performance that unfolds like a work of conceptual art . . . *Fairview*, a twenty-first-century play with a radical 1960s soul, deconstructs the warping power of the white gaze."

—CHARLES MCNULTY, *LA TIMES*

"It is easy for white people in theater, of which there are many, to talk about making room for nonwhite artists—writers, directors, actors, audience members. It is far more difficult to actually follow through with that. Making space requires sacrificing your own; listening requires shutting up. *Fairview* was actively concerned with how to make this happen: Drury's play articulated, first subtly and then less so, the way white audiences infringe on black artists telling their own stories . . . What began as a fairly broad comedy about the Frasier family coming together to celebrate their grandmother's birthday became a searing indictment of how challenging it is for white people like myself—however well intentioned—to not inflict our perspectives and biases on stories that don't belong to us. There are many ways that theater can have value, and one of them is not necessarily better than the others, but there is something particularly potent about theater that can make you feel this level of unease, especially if you are a member of a group who is rarely made to feel that way. Some plays succeed by giving you comfort; others succeed by getting under your skin."

—LOUIS PEITZMAN, *BUZZFEED NEWS*

"Hilarious, provocative, and disorienting . . . *Fairview* introduces us to an environment in which reality and personality crash at high speeds, like a theatrical Hadron Collider. Not since Branden Jacobs-Jenkins's *An Octoroon* has a play so thoroughly traversed the boundaries of race in performance, screwing with our perceptions while forcing us to recognize our blind spots."

—ZACHARY STEWART, *THEATERMANIA*

"A hugely intelligent play . . . a meticulously crafted, metatheatrical experiment in racial discourse . . . In larger society, such exercises in imagination seem near-impossible—but maybe, Drury suggests, rehearsing them onstage offers us a dose of the courage we need out in the real world."

—MIRIAM FELTON-DANSKY, *VILLAGE VOICE*

FAIRVIEW

FAIRVIEW

A Play

JACKIE SIBBLIES DRURY

THEATRE COMMUNICATIONS GROUP
NEW YORK
2019

Fairview is published by Theatre Communications Group, Inc.,
520 Eighth Avenue, 24th Floor, New York, NY 10018-4156

The publication of *Fairview* by Jackie Sibblies Drury, through TCG's Book Program, is made possible in part by the New York State Council on the Arts with the support of Governor Andrew Cuomo and the New York State Legislature.

Special thanks to Jujamcyn Theaters (Jordan Roth, President) for its generous support of this publication.

TCG books are exclusively distributed to the book trade by Consortium Book Sales and Distribution.

ISBN 978-1-55936-952-7 (paperback)
ISBN 978-1-55936-914-5 (ebook)
A catalog record for this book is available from the Library of Congress.

Book design and composition by Lisa Govan
Cover design by Naomi Usher, Studio Usher
Illustration by Adam Hayes & Tyler Sprangler; model is Kara Young

First Edition, July 2019

FAIRVIEW

PRODUCTION HISTORY

Fairview was originally commissioned and produced by Soho Rep. and Berkeley Repertory Theatre. *Fairview* had its world premiere at Soho Rep. (Sarah Benson, Artistic Director; Cynthia Flowers, Executive Director) in New York on June 17, 2018. It was directed by Sarah Benson. The scenic design was by Mimi Lien, the costume design was by Montana Levi Blanco, the lighting design was by Amith Chandrashaker, the sound design was by Mikaal Sulaiman, the choreography was by Raja Feather Kelly, the prop design was by Ryan Courtney, the hair and wig design was by Cookie Jordan; the fight director was J. David Brimmer, the dramaturg was Madeleine Oldham, the associate director was Garrett Allen, the production stage manager was Terri K. Kohler. The cast was:

BEVERLY	Heather Alicia Simms
DAYTON	Charles Browning
JASMINE	Roslyn Ruff
KEISHA	MaYaa Boateng
SUZE	Hannah Cabell
MACK	Jed Resnick
BETS	Natalia Payne
JIMBO	Luke Robertson

This production opened at Berkeley Repertory Theatre (Tony Taccone, Artistic Director; Susan Medak, Managing Director) on October 4, 2018. The creative team remained the same with the following changes: the stage manager was Leslie M. Radin. The cast also remained the same with the following changes:

BEVERLY	Natalie Venetia Belcon
JASMINE	Chantal Jean-Pierre
KEISHA	Monique Robinson
SUZE	Brooke Bloom

Fairview opened at Theatre for a New Audience (Jeffrey Horowitz, Founding Artistic Director; Dorothy Ryan, Managing Director; Robert E. Buckholz, Board Chair) on June 2, 2019. The cast and creative team were the same as the Soho Rep. production with the following change: the production stage manager was Shane Schnetzler.

CAST LIST

BEVERLY

DAYTON

JASMINE

KEISHA

Then:

SUZE

MACK

BETS

JIMBO

Then:

EVERYONE

ACTS

ACT ONE appears to be a comedic family drama.

ACT TWO watches Act One.

ACT TWO pushes further into Act One and tries to drive it forward to make Act Three.

A NOTE

Text in [brackets] is optional.

A QUOTE

"'Dirty nigger!' or simply 'Look! A Negro!'"
—From *Black Skin, White Masks*, Frantz Fanon

This, reversed, is the play, in a way.

ACT ONE

Lights up on a negro:
Beverly is peeling carrots, real carrots,
on a theater set that looks like a nice living/dining room
in a nice house in a nice neighborhood.
Music is playing.
Beverly lip-synchs to the song.
She dances and peels her carrots.
She dances and peels until the music from the speaker
goes a little funny.
There is a glitch of some kind.
It makes Beverly nervous.

Beverly glares at the speaker.
The speaker fixes itself.

Beverly thinks:
Everything is fine.
Everything is going to be perfect today.

And then Beverly does that thing:
she looks at herself in a pretend mirror hung on the fourth wall.
It's a very normal thing to have happen in a play.

Beverly checks hair, outfit, teeth, she looks good.
As she applies lipstick, she starts to dance again.
Dayton enters with a bunch of silverware.
He sees Beverly.

Dayton thinks:
Ooooh yes, my wife is a sexy woman.

Eventually Beverly feels herself being looked at.
She turns to discover Dayton, startled, she lets out a little cry:

BEVERLY: What are you looking at?!
DAYTON: You.
BEVERLY: Me?
DAYTON: That's right.
BEVERLY: You can't just sneak up on people, Dayton.
DAYTON: I can't sneak up on you, you're my wife.
BEVERLY: You say hello, you don't just watch a person.
DAYTON: Sneak up on—Beverly I live here.
BEVERLY: You don't just watch a person,
    and they don't know you're there,
    and you're just standing there just looking at them.
DAYTON: But what if I just like to look at you?
BEVERLY: Can't you look at me And say hello?
DAYTON: Uh-un. Not when you look as fine as you do.
BEVERLY: Oh, Dayton. You can be sweet when you want to,
    can't you.
DAYTON: Come over here and give me a kiss.
BEVERLY: But I'm so behind! If I don't get these carrots ready—

DAYTON: Beverly Frasier if you don't come over here and show me what you think of me—?

(She gives him a peck on the cheek, and flees.
He chases her, pulls her in for a bigger kiss.
She squeals.
They are close, and it's sweet.
But then she notices the silverware he brought.)

BEVERLY: And what do we have here?

DAYTON: Silverware.

BEVERLY: I asked for place settings for six.

And what did you bring me?

DAYTON: Six forks, six knives, six spoons.

BEVERLY: Dessert forks and butter knives and serving spoons.

What's a person supposed to eat with that?

DAYTON: . . . Food?

BEVERLY: Oh Dayton. This is Mama's birthday.

And she was already in a mood, when she went upstairs.

Everything must be perfect today.

DAYTON: Beverly. I am here. Here I am. Trying to help you.

BEVERLY: Help me lose my mind is what.

DAYTON: Trying to help you keep it.

So, tell me, woman: what do you want from me?

BEVERLY: I want . . . six forks, six knives, six spoons.

DAYTON: Alright, Beverly.

BEVERLY: I'm going to seat Mama here—

DAYTON: At the head of the table?

BEVERLY: It's her birthday.

DAYTON: It's my house.

BEVERLY: Our house. So, Mama. Me. Keisha. Tyrone. You.

And Jasmine.

DAYTON: You didn't tell me Jasmine's coming.

BEVERLY: Didn't I? Of course Jasmine is coming. She's my sister.

DAYTON: I thought you wanted this dinner to go well.

BEVERLY: Dayton, please.

DAYTON: That woman knows every thing about everybody
and never has one good thing to say about anybody.
She's a one-woman FBI NSA KGB.

BEVERLY: She's family. And family is / everything.

DAYTON: Everything. I know. Shut up Dayton and get
the silverware. I know.

(Dayton exits.)

BEVERLY: Thank you Dayton.
You're a big help.
And bring the root vegetables you bought!
I need to get them in the oven.
And the cheese plate!
Dayton?
You bought the root vegetables that I asked you to,
didn't you?!
Dayton?
Dayton!?!
How come he can hear me
when I'm not even talking to him,
but the second I ask him for something he can't hear a thing?

(A doorbell ring sound.)

Company's here!
Oh no! Company's here!
And I'm not ready.

(Beverly runs around in a last-minute scramble:)

Oh, I haven't even started the root vegetables,
they need at least an hour!

Oh no, Dayton!

Oh my lord.

Dayton, what did I say about putting beer on my coffee table?

(A doorbell ring sound.
She hides the beer bottle on the set.)

Like he doesn't care What we look like to people.

Dayton, where is the cheese plate?

Lord give me strength.

Dayton?!

Dayton!?

Dayton!?!!?!

(Dayton enters with the cheese plate.)

DAYTON: I'll answer the door. You finish up in the kitchen.

BEVERLY: Oh, I just wanted everything to go well today.

DAYTON: Everything's going to be fine. Don't worry.

(Beverly exits.
Jasmine enters with a bottle of rosé
and some flowers for Mama.)

JASMINE: Haaaaaaaaaaaaaay! How you doin' baby?

DAYTON: Oh, I'm fine, I'm fine, Jasmine.

JASMINE: Are you?

DAYTON: Yes, I'm doing well.

JASMINE: That's not what I heard.

DAYTON: Can I take that wine from you?

JASMINE: Yes, and put it in the freezer so it gets nice and cold, alright?

DAYTON: Got it. Why don't you help yourself to some cheese:

(Dayton presents the cheese plate.)

We have an Aged Gouda, a Humboldt Fog,
and some lovely Brie.

JASMINE: Oh wow.

I'm off dairy.

But that looks nice though, doesn't it.

DAYTON: I didn't know that.

JASMINE: Mmm-hmm. Can't you tell? I think I look like a snack.

DAYTON: Does Beverly know that?

JASMINE: Well. If my sister cared to know, then she would know.

DAYTON: Alright, Jasmine. Can I get you a glass of wine?

JASMINE: I want the wine I brought.

I'll wait.

(Dayton mimes an impression of Jasmine.
Jasmine turns to see it,
and he pretends to do something else, and exits.
Jasmine looks at herself in the pretend mirror
hung on the fourth wall.
Jasmine checks hair, outfit, teeth.
Eventually music restarts,
without anything onstage initiating it.
Jasmine looks around, like "um, what."
She decides to ignore it. She looks good.
But she's hungry. She eyes the cheese plate.
She looks around to see if anyone is watching.
She goes over and takes a bite of cheese.
From offstage:)

BEVERLY: Jasmine?! You better not be eating that cheese!

(Jasmine spits out the cheese, hides it on the set,
and poses, feigning calm.
Beverly enters.)

JASMINE: Oh, hello Beverly. That's a lovely outfit.

BEVERLY: Dairy free.

JASMINE: What? Oh yes.

I look good, don't I?

BEVERLY: Why do you always have to be

Just Like how you always are?

JASMINE: You know what?

BEVERLY: What.

JASMINE: . . . It's a special day.

I'm here for Mama's birthday.

She was a wonderful mother to you and me and Tyrone,

she has lived a long and illustrious life,

and I am not trying to disrespect that because you trippin'

over some budget Brie and some grapes.

BEVERLY: Jasmine.

JASMINE: Oh, come on girl.

You out here with some President Brie,

ain't cost more than three ninety-nine,

talkin' 'bout special cheese for Mama.

BEVERLY: Please don't start with me today.

JASMINE: I didn't start anything.

You're the one who summons us all to your house

like you the Queen of Sheba.

You're the one who walked in,

no hello, no how are you,

just on me right away about some three ninety-nine cheese.

Well.

I might feel some type of way about that.

That's all I'm saying.

BEVERLY: Today isn't about you. And it isn't about me.

It's about Mama.

JASMINE: I know exactly what today is about. Is she here?

BEVERLY: She's upstairs.

JASMINE: Well, let me go up and say hello.

BEVERLY: Oh, Jasmine, don't.

JASMINE: Why are you so nervous?

BEVERLY: I'm not nervous.

JASMINE: What is there to be nervous about?

BEVERLY: Nothing. I just want everything to go well.

JASMINE: It will.

BEVERLY: It has to. It just has to.

JASMINE: Beverly, you are going to give yourself a stroke if you
don't calm down.
Sit down. Have a glass of wine. I brought rosé.

BEVERLY: That does sound nice.

JASMINE: It's from France.

BEVERLY: I just put it in the fridge. Do you want a glass?

JASMINE: Why you put the wine in the fridge
when I said put it in the freezer.

BEVERLY: You didn't say to put the wine in the freezer.

JASMINE: I know what I said.

BEVERLY: . . . Let me get us a glass of wine.

JASMINE: Well, put an ice cube in it, since it's still warm.

BEVERLY: Alright Jasmine, alright.

(Beverly exits.)

JASMINE: You don't have to take a tone with me
after you get me all stressed.
And put the rest of the bottle in the freezer, so it gets cold.
You hear that Beverly?
Beverly!?!!?!
Damn. That woman never listens to anybody.

*(Jasmine sneaks back over to the cheese plate.
Keisha enters.)*

KEISHA: Hi Aunt Jasmine.

JASMINE: What the—?! Keisha? You startled me.

KEISHA: Oh, I'm sorry.

JASMINE: It's alright.

(They do their special Auntie-Niece greeting.)

How are you Keisha?

KEISHA: Well.

(Keisha speaks in a run-on-sentence while taking off her jacket and leaving it for someone else to pick up and looking through her backpack and eating some snacks and checking her phone and maybe none of those things but maybe all of them and also other things like she just does Everything That Teenagers Do.)

Practice ran over Again because Tanya was late Again
so Coach made everyone run a lap
for every minute she was late
and she was a full seventeen minutes late
so everyone had to run seventeen laps after practice
just because Tanya is obsessed with Jaden
which is insane because Jaden is stupid as hell
I'm sorry but he is
he's just dumb
but Tanya is obsessed with him
so she's late to practice every single day
and Erika and I are so frustrated
because we could be a really good team
if everyone would work as hard as I do
like if everyone could work as hard as Erika does
we could be a really good team
but instead it's all a waste of time
because we're just waiting and waiting
waiting for people like Tanya to show up and then
waiting to see what our punishment is
for Tanya showing up late
and it's like sometimes I feel like

I'm spending my whole entire life waiting for punishment
and what kind of a life is that
do you know what I mean Aunt Jasmine
like there has to be more to life than that, doesn't there?

JASMINE: Well—

KEISHA: Where's my mom?

JASMINE: In the kitchen.

KEISHA: Where's Dad?

JASMINE: Hiding from your mom.

KEISHA: Ok. Aunt Jasmine, I need to ask you something.

JASMINE: What's going on Keisha?

KEISHA: . . . Will you please talk to my mom about me
taking a year off before college?

JASMINE: Oh, Keisha.

KEISHA: Please, Aunt Jasmine? This is so important to me.

JASMINE: I know, I know.

KEISHA: Six honors or AP classes every year,
three varsity sports,
choir, debate, yearbook,
shall I go on?

JASMINE: You're a very accomplished young lady.

KEISHA: And I'm exhausted.
Now, don't get me wrong. I can't wait for college.
But my Soul is exhausted.
I need some time away so that I might replenish myself
and gain valuable life experience
if I am to truly flourish in academia.

JASMINE: That's very well-articulated, Keisha.

KEISHA: I know! But she just won't listen to me.

JASMINE: Your mother doesn't listen to me either.

KEISHA: Please say you'll at least mention that a gap year
is a good idea?
Please?

JASMINE: Alright, Keisha, alright.

(Keisha cheers and does a happy dance.)

KEISHA: I'm going to jump in the shower.

JASMINE: You better hurry up. Your mother is in a mood.

KEISHA: Yup yup yup. Back down in a flash.

[Thank you Aunt Jasmine, you're the best!]

(Keisha runs upstairs.
Beverly enters with three glasses of rosé.)

BEVERLY: Keisha?

Was that Keisha?

I need her to help me with the pie crust.

JASMINE: I can help you.

BEVERLY: No, that's alright. I can do it.

(Beat.)

JASMINE: You know, Keisha mentioned that
she might want to take a minute before college to—

BEVERLY: My daughter is going to college.

I went to college. You went to college.

Our mother went to college.

It's not a conversation.

JASMINE: I think your daughter might—

BEVERLY: Are you telling me how to raise my child?

JASMINE: Nope.

BEVERLY: You just bring this glass of wine to Mama.

JASMINE: Alright then.

Mama? Your favorite daughter is here!

I brought a rosé from France!

[It tastes like a beautiful black man I met in Marseille,
did I tell you about him, Mama? Ooooh . . .]

(Jasmine exits.
Beverly is alone. She picks up a carrot.
A phone ring sound.)

BEVERLY: Every time.
    Hello?
    Hi Tyrone.
    What do you mean your flight was rerouted?
    Oh my goodness.
    Well how long will it take you to get here?
    Oh my goodness.
    Tyrone I told you that you should have come in yesterday.
    You act like you're the only lawyer at that firm.
    I know. I'm sorry.
    It's just it's important that you're here, important to Mama.
    It's important to me too.
    Alright. Alright.
    Well, just hurry up and get here.

(Beverly hangs up the phone.
Dayton has entered.)

DAYTON: Who was that?
BEVERLY: My idiot brother.
DAYTON: What has Tyrone done now?
BEVERLY: He couldn't be bothered to get here early
    like I told him to, no,
    and now, he might not even make it to dinner.
    Oh, I just can't believe him.
    He never puts the family first. He always thinks of himself.
DAYTON: Beverly, calm down.
    This dinner is going to be wonderful,
    because you're a wonderful cook,
    and a wonderful host, and everyone here loves you.

BEVERLY: You're right. You're right Dayton.
Did you bring me those root vegetables?

DAYTON: Um—

BEVERLY: Oh, Dayton, Don't Tell Me you didn't pick up the root
vegetables.

DAYTON: I—

BEVERLY: I told you that I needed assorted root vegetables.

DAYTON: Wuh—

BEVERLY: I said assorted root vegetables
and you said what's a root vegetable
and I said anything that grows underground
and you said like what
and I said just look in the store and think about it
and get some of what looks good
and you said oh no no no,
I need specific instructions so that I don't do the wrong thing
oh no, you said
and so I said, fine,
I need four parsnips, four sweet potatoes, a turnip, a beet,
and a celeriac
and you said what's a celeriac
and I said a celery root
and you said what's a celery root
and I showed you a picture
and you said that looks nasty
and I said it just looks like a root
and you said carrots don't look like that
and I said they would without genetic modification
and then we argued about the industrialization of agriculture
and its effects on our concept of what food is supposed to
look like
and after that argument I said
do you want me to write you a list of the root vegetables
I need
and you said no, you don't need to write this stuff down

and I said are you sure
and you said Beverly, I don't need to write anything down
and I said ok, but do you want me to remind you
and you said you treat me like some kind of fool
and I kept my mouth shut.
And I thought I should remember to remind him anyway
and I knew that I should have reminded you
I said to myself you should remind him
and then I said to myself oh, you don't need to remind him,
he's a grown man, he knows what he said he'd do,
he knows how important this is to me,
he knows everything about this dinner needs to be perfect.
And Then you come in here and—
DAYTON *(Presenting the root vegetables)*: Ta-da!

(Beat.)

BEVERLY: One day, I will kill you.
DAYTON: Not today.
BEVERLY: Do you hear me?
I will murder you, one day, mark my words.

(A timer beep sound.)

Oooh! That's the short ribs! Dayton, that's the short ribs.
DAYTON: I got it.
BEVERLY: Don't take it out.
DAYTON: Don't take it out?
BEVERLY: Just turn the oven up to four fifty,
    and set the timer for ten minutes.
DAYTON: Don't take it out.
BEVERLY: No. Four fifty, ten minutes.
DAYTON: Four fifty, ten minutes.
BEVERLY: I'm going to peel these vegetables.
DAYTON: 1-2-3 Go Team!

BEVERLY: Yes, four fifty, ten minutes.

DAYTON: Alright, Bev. Alright.

(Dayton exits.
Beverly is alone.
A door slam sound.)

JASMINE *(From offstage)*: Mama open the door.
Mama?
Fine. Be like that.

(Jasmine reenters.)

That woman has lost the little bit [of sense]
that God gave her.

BEVERLY: Oh, Jasmine, what did you do.

JASMINE: Me? I didn't do anything.
All I did was say hello,
and Mama just went and locked herself in the bathroom.

BEVERLY: Oh my goodness.

JASMINE: I'm not even worried about it.

BEVERLY: Oh my goodness.

JASMINE: It's just Mama being Mama.
Always wants to be in the center of everything.

BEVERLY: If Mama doesn't enjoy this birthday dinner, then—

JASMINE: Then what?

BEVERLY: I don't know. Jasmine, I just don't know.

JASMINE: Let her lock herself upstairs.
The second she thinks that we're not talking about her,
she'll come down.

BEVERLY: I hope so, Jasmine. I hope so.

JASMINE: And you know our brother is the same way.
Do whatever he need to do to be at the center of attention.
Crazy-ass Geminis.

Every single person in this family is so full of drama
I don't even know how I stand it.

BEVERLY: I don't have drama.

JASMINE: Girl you got drama.
Tyrone drama, Mama drama,
you all are like one of those movies.

BEVERLY: What movies.

JASMINE: Like, a family drama.

BEVERLY: What do you mean?

JASMINE: Like a movie.

BEVERLY: What movie?

JASMINE: Come on, girl, you know what I'm saying.
You know, one of those movies that's a family drama:
Where somebody dead, and what to do with the children
or somebody dead and what to do with the wife
or somebody dead and the house ain't paid for,
and there's all these people that try to help
but she can't take the help
and things get worse, and they try to help
but she can't take the help
and things get worse,
until, finally, she takes the help
that they all have been trying to give her
for the whole damn movie,
so that she get the kid
or get the kid to dance
or get the dog
or get the dog to dance.
And then they all walk on down to the water,
with a new shirt on,
and the breeze is blowing,
and they all look out at that water,
and talk about how they're not better,
not yet,
but they're starting to be.

Mmm, mmm, mmm.

Yes, girl, a good old family drama.

A slice of life.

I love those movies.

You know, nothing big and flashy,

just watching real stories about real people.

BEVERLY: Nothing real about those kinds of movies.

Those kinds of things just don't happen in real life.

JASMINE: Don't even try to start an argument with me,

what is wrong with you,

can I live?

BEVERLY: We are nothing like the people in those movies.

JASMINE: Can't I just talk about something? Damn.

BEVERLY: Well, if you're sitting there and talking,

it means that I have to stand here and listen to you.

JASMINE: Fine. I won't say one thing to you.

BEVERLY: Fine.

(Beat.)

JASMINE *(To herself)*: Just trying to make some conversation

about some nice uplifting movies

and she's trying to tell me that:

that doesn't happen to people.

(Sucks teeth)

Like nobody know somebody that's dead

or got a new dog in their whole life:

that doesn't happen that's not true.

Please.

BEVERLY: That's not what I meant.

JASMINE: I. Am not talking. To you. Ok?

(Continuing to herself:)

Having a private-ass conversation with myself

thinking through my own damn thoughts

and she trying to tell me

that what I am thinking to myself is wrong.
I'm not even talking to her.
Why she got to have an opinion
about every damn thought in my head
like, damn,
let me think something stupid if I want to for a minute,
what does it even matter?
And I'm not even being stupid, I'm just thinking to myself,
and if I want to be stupid when I'm just thinking to myself,
what is it to you? Huh?
Like if I want to think about something stupid, to myself,
by myself,
what is that to you?
Like if I want to think that Beverly is uppity,
and she like to put on like she better than everybody,
but everybody know she cheap as shit,
and I want to say that to myself
and not say that to anybody else,
then what's the problem with that?
Huhn? You got anything to say?
You better not because I'm not even talking to you.
Damn.
She not that bad.
Beverly's not that bad.
She's just all pent up because her man don't love her right.

BEVERLY: Jasmine.

JASMINE *(To herself)*: He don't know how to move right,
you can see it from how he walk.
Walk around like his balls all heavy. Balls ain't that heavy.
Unless he got some kind of illness or something.
Is Dayton sick?

BEVERLY: Are you talking to me, Jasmine?

JASMINE: Yeah. Is Dayton sick?

BEVERLY: No.

JASMINE: Well that's good.

But, then, why aren't you two gettin'—

BEVERLY: That. Is. None of your business.

JASMINE: You make it my business when you're acting all crazy.

BEVERLY: I am not acting any type of way.

JASMINE: Mmmhmm.

BEVERLY: I'm not.

JASMINE: Mmmmmm-hmmmm.

BEVERLY: What?

(Keisha enters, dancing.)

KEISHA: I'm clean! And I'm starving! I feel so great!

(This repeats as necessary:
She's doing a dance where she smells her armpits and rubs her tummy.)

JASMINE: What is that.

KEISHA: It's my I'm clean and I'm starving dance.

JASMINE: You get that from your grandmother.

That woman has a dance for everything.

You remember her birthday dance Beverly?

BEVERLY: . . . The gown.

JASMINE: That Gown.

BEVERLY: The turban.

JASMINE: That Turban.

Oooh Keisha, your grandmother was something back in the day.

BEVERLY: Her birthday outfit was a gown,

JASMINE: an Ivory gown,

BEVERLY: an Ivory gown with golden threads sewn through it.

JASMINE: And a Golden turban,

BEVERLY: Golden turban,

JASMINE: with a big ol' diamond rhinestone at the center.
And she'd work her hands like this,
like charming the snakes out the gates,
BEVERLY: and her nails would be all,
JASMINE: and she would slither. And then pose.
BEVERLY: And slither. And then pose.
JASMINE: And work her nails. And work her eyes.
And she'd say *(Singing or talking, or some variation)*
Oooooo, all the men.
JASMINE AND BEVERLY *(Singing or talking, or some variation)*:
Oooooo, all the boys
Oooooo, let them see me
Oooooo, let them see me.
DAYTON *(Entering)*: Mama Frasier Birthday Dance!
JASMINE, BEVERLY AND DAYTON: Oooooo, the women
Oooooo, the lil' dolls
Oooooo, let them see me
Oooooo, let them see me.

(Keisha joins in.)

JASMINE, BEVERLY, DAYTON AND KEISHA: Oooooo, I look good
Oooooo, I know I'm good
Oooooo, let them see it
Oooooo, pray them see it.

*(Keisha looks out toward us and has a soliloquy,
which is a theatrical device where a character talks aloud
and no one onstage can hear them.)*

KEISHA: It's all just . . . so beautiful!
I love these women.
Joy. And Dancing and Singing!
My future just looks so big and bright,
I can't wait for it to hurry up and Get Here.
I want to know all there is to know and be all there is to be.

But.

But I feel like something is keeping me from all that.

Something . . .

Yes, something is keeping me from what I could be.

And that something.

It thinks that it has made me who I am.

It's . . . It's just so confusing.

(A phone ring sound.)

DAYTON: Keisha?

KEISHA: What is it, Dad?

DAYTON: Telephone.

KEISHA: For me?

DAYTON: Yes.

(Keisha exits with phone.)

BEVERLY: Dayton, is everything ready?

DAYTON: Yep.

BEVERLY: Got the real napkins?

DAYTON: Yes.

BEVERLY: Napkin rings?

DAYTON: Yes.

BEVERLY: Water glasses and wine glasses?

DAYTON: Yes.

BEVERLY: Salad fork dinner fork dessert fork steak knife
butter knife soup spoon tea
spoon?

DAYTON: Believe so.

BEVERLY: Alright.

(Beat.)

Candles!!!? Did we get Candles?!?

DAYTON: Yes.

BEVERLY: Oh. Good. Everything's going to be fine.

(Keisha enters.)

Who was that?

KEISHA: It's nothing Mom. It was just Erika.

BEVERLY: And what does she want.

KEISHA: She just wants to drop something off.

BEVERLY: What.

KEISHA: I don't know. Something . . . for school.

BEVERLY: Mmm-hmmm.

KEISHA: An assignment . . . What?

BEVERLY: Keisha, I don't want your little friend coming over here
and interrupting this dinner.

KEISHA: Mom, you need to relax.

BEVERLY: You know your grandmother doesn't like that Erika.

KEISHA: Grandma doesn't have a problem with her.

BEVERLY: Oh, your grandmother has a problem with how you
two are together,
you better believe that.

KEISHA: . . .

BEVERLY: Now she won't say that to you,
because she wants her granddaughter to love her,
but your grandmother is a woman with some opinions. Yes.
That woman has some opinions.

KEISHA: . . .

JASMINE: Keisha, come on over here and sit with your aunt.

BEVERLY: Keisha doesn't need to talk to you right now, Jasmine.
What Keisha needs to do is to go on in that kitchen,
and check on her grandmother's birthday cake,
and help her mother out today.
That's what Keisha needs to do.

KEISHA: Fine.

(Keisha exits.)

BEVERLY: And don't you stomp in my house
if you want to keep living here.

JASMINE: Beverly, you need to calm down. Can't you see—

BEVERLY: If I don't finish chopping these carrots,
    I am going to lose it.

DAYTON: Bev, I think you better put that knife down.

BEVERLY: If I don't chop these carrots, who's gonna chop them?
    Hmmn? You?

DAYTON: Put the knife down, Bev.

JASMINE: Beverly, why don't you sit down and have a drink.

BEVERLY: I'm fine.

DAYTON: You are clearly not fine.

JASMINE: What is wrong with you?

KEISHA *(From offstage)*: Mom?! I think the cake is burnt.

BEVERLY: *(Gasp)*

JASMINE: Uh-oh.

BEVERLY *(Whispered or silent)*: Nooo!!!

DAYTON: Bev, it'll be fine—

JASMINE: Dayton will run out and buy a cake—

BEVERLY: I can fix it.

JASMINE: Won't you Dayton?

BEVERLY: I can fix it.

DAYTON: I'll be happy to get a cake!

BEVERLY: I can fix it.

JASMINE: Why don't you just sit down and I'll get you some wine.

BEVERLY: I can fix it! Alright? Everything is fine!
    Everything will be just—

(Beverly pauses, looking glassy.
Beverly faints, spilling carrots all over the floor.
Jasmine and Dayton gasp in horror.
Keisha runs in.)

KEISHA: Mom? Mom!

END OF ACT ONE

ACT TWO

Lights up on a negro:
Beverly is peeling carrots, real carrots,
on a theater set that looks like a nice living/dining room
in a nice house in a nice neighborhood.

Music is playing.
Beverly lip-synchs to the song.
She dances and peels her carrots.
She dances and peels until the music from the speaker
goes a little funny.
There is a glitch of some kind.
It makes Beverly nervous.

Beverly glares at the speaker.
The speaker fixes itself.

We hear the following conversation,
and it begins in medias res, rapidly, conversationally,
with overlapping text and ad-libbed reactions, stutters, and sounds.

I've included stage directions from Act One to give a sense of the tim-
ing that we found in the Soho Rep./Berkeley Rep productions.
But you do you.

SUZE: No no no no no.

JIMBO: No, but if you could choose to be a different race,
  what race would you be?
  Do you know what I mean?

SUZE: No, I do, but,

JIMBO: No, but like,
  like if you could choose to be any race you want,
  any race at all,
  like if you could choose to be any race at all,
  what race would you be? Because like,

SUZE: no, right,

JIMBO: yeah, I think it's an interesting question.

SUZE: no, sure, it might be, some day,

JIMBO: It's definitely interesting.

SUZE: no, yeah.

JIMBO: Because I think about things like that.
  Do you know what I mean?

SUZE: Yeah, yeah.

JIMBO: I actually like to think, like to think about things,
  you know?

SUZE: Yeah, me too.

JIMBO: Like, if you could choose to be a different race,
  what race would you choose?

(Dayton enters onstage.)

SUZE: I don't think you know what you mean,
    do you know what I mean?

JIMBO: What?

SUZE: Like, do you see what you're asking?

JIMBO: What do you mean?

SUZE: Like, I don't think you're really looking at what you're talking about, do you see what I'm saying?

JIMBO: Oh, come on.

SUZE: Like I wouldn't. I just wouldn't.

JIMBO: You wouldn't choose to be anything?

SUZE: No, I would never.

JIMBO: Why not?

SUZE: Well, because you just can't change something like that.

JIMBO: Why not?

SUZE: Well, because race isn't something you can change.
    I mean, obviously.

JIMBO: I thought you said race is a construct.

SUZE: It is.

JIMBO: So.

SUZE: So just because it's a construct doesn't mean that it isn't real, like that's not.

JIMBO: Well, that just doesn't make any sense at all.

SUZE: So, if you could choose, what race would you be?

JIMBO: If I could choose I would be Asian.

SUZE: Ok. Wow.

JIMBO: What?

SUZE: No, just you said that so quickly.

JIMBO: Well, I've thought about it before.

SUZE: You've thought about it before.

JIMBO: Of course I've thought about it before.

SUZE: So, like why would you want to be Asian?

JIMBO: I mean, is there something wrong with being Asian?

SUZE: No, oh my god, there's nothing wrong with being an Asian person. Oh my god.

JIMBO: I mean, I don't think there's anything wrong with being
Asian, but.

SUZE: I just meant to ask. Wait wait wait.
I just meant to ask why the Asian race is the race
that you would choose, if you could.
Do you know what I mean?

JIMBO: Right right right.

SUZE: I mean, this is your question. I don't.

JIMBO: I see what you mean.

SUZE: Yeah.

JIMBO: Because, from what I've learned,
it can be a really . . . traditional culture.

SUZE: Being Asian can.

JIMBO: Yeah, definitely.

SUZE: Huh.

JIMBO: I've come to understand that it's a traditional culture,
just from what I've read, and,
you know, from girls I've dated.

SUZE: Huh.

JIMBO: Yeah.

SUZE: Yeah.

JIMBO: Yeah, there are a lot of expectations.
Like, there's just so much that's expected
of children from their parents.
There is so much pressure.
Yeah, pressure to excel, pressure to conform.
Asian parents are just like,
You must do this, or you can't do that.
So, if I were Asian, I wouldn't participate
in that whole system.
You know?

SUZE: Like what.

JIMBO: I'd do what's unexpected.

SUZE: Like what?

JIMBO: Like I'd be Asian but I'd be rebellious,

SUZE: Ok.

JIMBO: like I'd be Asian but I'd be loud,

SUZE: Yeah.

JIMBO: and difficult,

SUZE: Yeah.

JIMBO: and fucking impolite, you know?

SUZE: Yeah.

JIMBO: Like, Asian people don't have to be just this one thing,

SUZE: Right, but.

JIMBO: like, actually, that they can be a million things.

SUZE: Right.

JIMBO: Do you know what I mean?

SUZE: I have literally no idea what you're talking about.

JIMBO: Don't you know any Asian people?

SUZE: I do, of course.

JIMBO: So don't you feel like they're all like so pent up?

SUZE: No, I don't.

JIMBO: Like they're all just repressed?

SUZE: No, I don't know.

JIMBO: I mean, every Asian I know is like tortured
by their parents' expectations.

SUZE: I don't feel comfortable making some huge statement
about every—

JIMBO: Oh, I don't feel comfortable.

SUZE: I don't. Just grouping people—

JIMBO: Right, because you're a good little liberal,

SUZE: what?

JIMBO: so you just want to pretend that you're cool
with everyone,

SUZE: I'm not—

JIMBO: cool with every race, cool with every culture,

SUZE: I'm not—

JIMBO: you're like, Hello world, welcome, I value your culture,

SUZE: I'm not—

JIMBO: and because your culture is different than mine, I don't judge it at all.

SUZE: But I'm not—

JIMBO: You're not what?

SUZE: But I'm not Asian. So. I don't know what it's like to—

JIMBO: So just because someone is Asian they deserve to have a fucked-up relationship with their family?

SUZE: I.

JIMBO: Like they deserve that?

SUZE: Ok. First.

I think it is crazy to say that every Asian person has a fucked-up relationship with their family.

JIMBO: No, but—

SUZE: Like that is a Crazy thing to say. Right?

JIMBO: Sure, but—

SUZE: Like you hear how that sounds, right?

JIMBO: Alright, Calm Down. Hear me out.

Because, ok, If I were Asian, do you know what I would do?

SUZE: What.

JIMBO: I would take my parents to therapy.

SUZE: . . . Ok.

JIMBO: We'd go to group therapy.

And we'd talk about our like dependency issues or whatever.

SUZE: So.

JIMBO: And I'd be like, Hey, Mom and Dad,

aren't we all happier now?

And they'd be like,

Yes, Son, we are happier now.

SUZE: Ok.

JIMBO: And then I'd be like: hey all other Asians,

SUZE: Oh boy.

JIMBO: look at me, I'm a happy Asian guy. With a happy mom and a happy dad.

SUZE: Yeah.

JIMBO: Like, I did whatever the fuck I wanted to do,

SUZE: Right.

JIMBO: and then they got mad, like Asian parents do—

SUZE: Sorry, can I stop you for a second?

JIMBO: What's up.

SUZE: I think I just need you to stop talking for a second.

JIMBO: Why?

SUZE: Because I'm getting really uncomfortable.

JIMBO: ["What is your problem?"]

SUZE: [I'm sorry, but can you just shut the—shut up?]

JIMBO: [Um. Ok.]

SUZE: [Yeah, thank you.]

JIMBO: [Yeah, you're welcome.]

SUZE: [Yeah, I said thank you, thanks.]

JIMBO: [And I said you're welcome.]

Jasmine enters onstage.

MACK: Soooooooo. What are we talking about. What's going on.
Wait, is something happening?
JIMBO: I have posed a hypothetical question.
SUZE: Ugh.
MACK: Reeeallly.
JIMBO: It has rankled some,
SUZE: I can't.
MACK: Intriguing.
JIMBO: But I would like to pose it to you, if you, uh, consent.
SUZE: Literally the worst.
MACK: I do. What is it?
JIMBO: Alright.

(Dayton presents the cheese plate.)

If you could choose to be a different race,
what race would you be?

MACK: Are we asking about race or ethnicity?

JIMBO: Yeah, if you could be a different race or ethnicity,
what would you be.

MACK: Like, would I have to be that race all the time?

JIMBO: Yeah you'd have to be that race 24/7.

MACK: I see.

JIMBO: Right.

MACK: Would I have like grown up as that race?

JIMBO: Um.

MACK: Or would I like,

JIMBO: Yeah.

MACK: just turn into that race like right now?

JIMBO: Let's say that you're you,

MACK: Ok.

JIMBO: but then you like magically become—

MACK: Magically?

JIMBO: Like you just wake up one morning
and you're a different race. Right?

MACK: And it's like in today's world,

JIMBO: Yes.

MACK: it's not in the past.

JIMBO: No. So, what would you be?

(Jasmine looks at herself in the "mirror.")

MACK: It's interesting, you know?
Like if I was going to like Become a different race,
and I could choose that.
It would be like . . . I mean based on what criteria,
you know?
Like if I just think about, like,
would I want to choose a race
that is more like who I actually am?

To express something essential about myself?

OR would I want to choose a race that is totally different
from who I actually am.

To like, try something new.

I feel like I would want to try something that expresses
more of who I am, maybe.

Like on the surface
sometimes I think people think I'm boring,
but actually, like my true self is this like wild person.
[You know, like I have this hot, muggy river of
uncut sensuality flowing deep down in my soul. So.]
Yeah, If I could choose to be a different race,
I'd want to be Latinx.

(Beverly enters.)

SUZE: Why would you be Latino?

MACK: Is there something wrong with being Latinx?

SUZE: No, oh my god,

I don't mean there's anything wrong with being Latino,
I'm just trying to ask why you're choosing to be Latino.

MACK: Latinx.

SUZE: Right, of course.

MACK: Well, because, honestly,

I just think it would be so fucking major to be Latinx.

Like to just get to be this fiery—

SUZE: No, I mean like— Do you speak Spanish?

MACK: Oh. No. Do you?

SUZE: I don't, but—

MACK: But it's like, I would love to speak Spanish. Obviously.

SUZE: Me too, but—

MACK: I keep doing this app, but it's not working.

SUZE: Oh.

MACK: I think it's hard without having people to practice with.

SUZE: Right, but—

MACK: And besides they say it's best to learn from conversation.

SUZE: Right, but—

MACK: Or, from, like, taking a lover.

SUZE: Right, but—

MACK: I would love to take A Latinx Lover.

SUZE: But you've traveled to—

MACK: Where?

SUZE: To, like, Latin . . . you know . . .

MACK: Oh, right I see.

SUZE: Right.

MACK: I have not.

SUZE: Ok, so, I'm trying to understand,

MACK: What's the matter?

SUZE: yeah, why would you choose to be, you know, Latinx?
Do you know what I mean?
Like, if you don't speak the language,
and you've never been there,
what about it is appealing to—

MACK: Well, excuse me for even having an opinion.

SUZE: Oh, no, I don't mean that—

MACK: Like, excuse me for not being as cultured as you.

SUZE: No, I'm just curious.

MACK: You know, I'm not like you, ok?

SUZE: I'm just curious—

MACK: I didn't grow up with like Money to like Travel.

SUZE: I didn't grow up with money to—

MACK: Yeah, I didn't grow up with money to go to like
Language Immersion Summer Camp, or whatever.

SUZE: I didn't—

MACK: Like, I haven't actually left the country,

SUZE: I didn't—

MACK: except to go to like, Canada once,
which isn't even a different country,

SUZE: I'm sorry—

MACK: except politically.

SUZE: I'm sorry—

MACK: I know you are sweetie, it's fine.

SUZE: I'm sorry—

MACK: I'm not mad, I'm just passionate.

SUZE: Ok—

MACK: Because it's like, you know that you don't have to go to another country to experience Latinx people and culture,

SUZE: Of course not,

MACK: it's not like you have to like go to some like village or something.

SUZE: of course not.

MACK: They are in Our country too.

SUZE: Of course.

MACK: And that's what's amazing—it's like because they're here, it's like their identity is being made here.

Like, most people are just what they are,

you're like, oh, that person is black that person is Asian,

but with Latinx people it's like,

they don't think, they just are what they are,

like this pelvic, spicy, bright bold thing,

they're like making it right now

and it's intersecting with gender

in like this amazing way, that is really really really . . .

it's just politically good, you know?

[. . . And not just politically good, it's like

muy caliente in the streets and in the sheets,

know what I'm sayin'?]

Keisha enters onstage.

BETS: So what are you talking about?

MACK: Ohmigod.

Thank god you're here.

I can't wait to hear how you're going to answer.

BETS: Me?

MACK: Yes. Ready?

BETS: For what?

MACK: Ok, they're asking:

If you could choose to be a different race,

what race would you choose?

. . . Do you understand the question?

BETS: Yes.

MACK: So what do you think.

BETS: But I am frustrated by this question.

MACK: But it's like you can choose—

BETS: Because, I—no, let me finish—
I need to talk to know what are my thoughts.
MACK: Sorry.
BETS: Because this question,
it is everything that is wrong with America.
In any other place this question would be a question that is
fun and charming to consider,
but in America, this question, what race,
it is a very boring question,
because everything in America is race, race, race,
all the people talk is race, race, race,
and no people are saying nothing new about race,
so with this question, "what race can you choose, what
race do you want?"
the question is interesting, maybe,
but the answer is boring, because it must be always the same.
Always: oh, race is not important, I have no opinion,
teach me.
Or: oh, my guilt, oh, I feel so bad, and I earn the—
the problem of that race, it is mine.
I deserve this.
You say nothing, or You say sorry.
That is all that you can say in this country.
It is so boring.
I have nothing to say.
[I have nothing to say.]
[Yes, I have absolutely nothing to say.]
MACK: Oh.
BETS: Unless.
MACK: What?
BETS: Hmm.
MACK: Unless what.
BETS: Unless, I can change my race to be.
Something that is interesting, maybe, is to be a Slav.
MACK: I'm sorry, what?

BETS: A Slav. It is the same in English, no?

MACK: I don't know what that is.

BETS: You don't have this: Slav?

MACK: No I don't think so.

BETS: Coming from Serbia, or some place like that.

Slovenia, Slovakia [Bosnia, Bulgaria, Belarus] . . .

MACK: Oh, ok.

BETS: Because, well, we travel a lot,

and when I was a girl, we went to there on holiday.

MACK: To Slovenia.

BETS: To all of them, all around. We travel a lot.

MACK: Wow.

BETS: It is quite lovely in these places.

The landscape in these places—

flat flat flat, just, you look and a what, a boulder,

with a little snow.

That is all that is there.

MACK *(Sotto voce)*: Oohhh.

BETS: But in that, it gives a point to look at,

and if you focus, you see the sky and it is beautiful.

MACK *(Sotto voce)*: Yaaas.

BETS: And the people, living all together in their little houses.

Their life is difficult, but they have so much, so much joy.

It is inspiring, no?

MACK: Mmmm.

BETS: I think so, yes.

MACK: Mmmmmm.

BETS: They are so proud, these people.

MACK: Wooow.

BETS: The strength of the personality that comes out of that place.

It is very, um, very pleasing to me.

To have that.

[A strong peasant soul.

Ah, so beautiful, don't you think?]

MACK: But . . . aren't they . . . um.

BETS: What is the question?

MACK: Are those people a different race than you are?

BETS: Of course.

MACK: They are a different race.

BETS: Of course.

MACK: Yes. Of course. It's just, I wouldn't have . . .

BETS: Tell me.

MACK: I just wouldn't have categorized you and them differently
that's all.

BETS: Well, that is ridiculous.

MACK: Right.

BETS: The food is different, the culture is different,
the look of the people is different.

MACK: Right.

BETS: That is what race is, no?

MACK: No, you're right.

BETS: Americans are obsessed with race.

MACK: You're right.

BETS: Obsessed.

MACK: You're right.

BETS: But they don't know what this is.

MACK: Totally.

BETS: You think Slav is not a race?

MACK: No it is. They are. It is.

BETS: Of course it is.

MACK: No, you're right.

BETS: [So, I choose Slav.]
[Oooh, or maybe I choose Turk.
A Turk can be fun. Or maybe too strange.]
[No, I will be Slav.
Slav is strange enough.]

Jasmine exits and Beverly starts to peel carrots.

SUZE *(To Bets)*: I'm sorry, but no.
BETS: What.
SUZE: That's crazy.
BETS: What is crazy.
SUZE: That's just. Choosing to be a different European race
    isn't choosing to be a different race.
    Obviously.

(Beverly picks up the phone.)

JIMBO: But you haven't answered.
    Everyone else has answered.
    I asked you, first, and you've talked shit
    about every other answer.
SUZE: I haven't talked anything—

JIMBO: But you haven't picked anything for yourself.
You're just avoiding the question.

SUZE: I'm not avoiding the—

JIMBO: So. If you could choose to be a different race, what would
you choose?

SUZE: Well.

JIMBO: If you know so much about everything,
what would you choose?

SUZE: I'd be African-American.

JIMBO: Oh, ho ho.

SUZE: For different reasons than anyone has.

JIMBO: Really.

SUZE: Yeah.
I'd be African-American.

JIMBO: Bullshit. I call bullshit.

SUZE: Why are you saying that.

JIMBO: Because it's fucking hard to be African-American,
and I don't think you really mean it.

SUZE: I do mean it.

JIMBO: So, if I like kidnapped you, and locked you in a room,
and like dyed your skin.

SUZE: That would not make me African-American.

JIMBO: If I did that, what you'd be stoked?

SUZE: That's not what it would be like.

JIMBO: So you'd be stoked.

SUZE: That's not—that's offensive and not—

JIMBO: Oh! So you wouldn't be stoked?

SUZE: No, if you Kidnapped me,
and like spray-painted me with like Dye,
no, no that wouldn't make me super happy.
Because that would be traumatizing.

JIMBO: I know but—

SUZE: And I can't even believe that I am saying this but,
like being African-American isn't like just dyeing your skin.

JIMBO: I know but—

SUZE: And it's like,
    I would choose to be African-American, actually.
    Because I was raised by.
    My family, we had a . . . but she was more than that,
    she was this lovely . . .
    Her name . . .
    (Quavering:)
    Her name was Mabel.
    And she . . .
    I'm sorry.
    I just loved her.
    Because, my parents,
    [they were great—they're great parents, but]
    I can see now that they were . . . reserved.
    But when I was a kid,
    I . . . couldn't understand why they didn't.
    Anyway.
    The person in my life who expressed love to me
    in a way that I could feel it,
    that was Mabel.
    She was the person who was there
    when I got home from school,
    she was the person who was there for me
    when I was sick or when I was hurt,
    she was the person who would play games with me
    and who I'd talk to about boys.
    Mabel was my person.
    It's like, she made everything I ate
    until I was like in college, basically.
    It's like, I grew up eating corn bread and collard greens.
    Like food that regular people don't even eat,
    you know?
    [Like I grew up on that kind of food.]
    Because it's like,
    if that's what ties you to a person,

food and love and feeling like,
if that's the thing that bonds you to a person,
if that's what helps you to be what you're meant to be,
if that's how you're raised.
Like the things from your childhood:
the people, the food, the culture of your . . .
you know . . . I just, I feel like she is my family.
Mabel is my . . . she's my mom.
She's my heart.
And that's . . .
It's complex.

(With Dayton's "Ta-da!")

JIMBO: But it wouldn't just be you being black with what's her
name, Mabel?
SUZE: Don't say her name like that. You don't get to—
JIMBO: It's not like you'd go black for Mabel
and then be normal the rest of the time.
SUZE: What is your point.
JIMBO: You'd be black 24/7.
SUZE: So?
JIMBO: So.
SUZE: So?
JIMBO: So. What would you do?
SUZE: What do you mean?
JIMBO: If I were black, I'd like live in it, and I'd experience it.
SUZE: Of course I'd experience it too.
JIMBO: I wouldn't just like hide in my childhood hidey-hole,
or some shit.
SUZE: I wouldn't try to hide anything.
JIMBO: So what would you do?
SUZE: Well. I mean, I'd try to help people!
JIMBO: Oooh! She'd help people!?
SUZE: Of course I'd try to help people. With life skills.

You know, fiscal responsibility,
and family planning,
or like retirement planning, like setting up a 401(k),
things we take for granted,
how to go on a job interview, how to get a mortgage.

JIMBO: Sounds fun!

SUZE: Well, not everything is fun.

JIMBO: Woo-fucking-hoo.

SUZE: Inherited poverty isn't very fun.

(Jasmine enters.)

MACK: But you know, not all black people are poor.
Like.
There are plenty of rich black people.

SUZE: I know.

BETS: Like Michael Jackson. He is very very rich.

MACK: Well . . . yes. Yes, he was.

BETS: And the other one. The sports guy.

MACK: There are a lot of—

BETS: The famous one. You know.

MACK: Ok . . . Do you mean like . . . Michael Jordan?

BETS: No, not that one.

MACK: Like . . . Magic Johnson?

BETS: No, not this Michael Jackson–sounding names.

MACK: I don't know, there are a lot of famous black athletes.

BETS: But Very famous, very rich.
This is an interesting kind of black to be.

MACK: Hmmm. Like . . .

BETS: The one . . .
The one who kill her wife.

MACK: Oh.
Do you mean . . . O.J. Simpson?

BETS: Yes! Oh, yes. He is very very rich.

MACK: Yes. He was.

BETS: And very funny.

MACK: I guess he was. Before the whole—

BETS: Of course, before, before.

Did you see this movie?

MACK: What movie?

BETS: Oh, this is a very funny movie:

O.J. Simpson is chased by all the people,

he is with the police and they chase him and chase him.

MACK: It's a movie though? Because that sounds like—

BETS: No, no it is a movie, yes, they chase and chase and chase

and they beat him up,

and he is very hurt, in the hospital,

and it is so funny, in the hospital he tells the man

that they chase him for drugs, they hurt him for drugs,

you know, common story for these people, it is obvious,

but he is in the hospital,

so the man think he is asking for drugs

because he have pain,

and the man give the, um—he press the button,

and O.J. say, "No! Wait! Listen!" and he lay back like.

SUZE: I don't think that is O.J. Simpson.

You're clearly thinking of a different African-American actor.

It's something called Racial Blindness.

It's like if you aren't raised around people of a certain race,

your brain is less—

you're not able to distinguish individual features,

so you're more likely to confuse different people of the

same race.

BETS: It is O.J. Simpson in this movie. Maybe I don't say it well,

my English—

SUZE: It's not your fault, it's Racial Blindness.

BETS: I don't have that.

SUZE: It's why lots of people mistake one African-American for

another—

BETS: I don't have that.

SUZE: I'm not saying you're racist.

BETS: The Juice Is Loose, I know O.J. Simpson.

I am not confused. He is a very rich black person.

SUZE: Fine.

BETS: [You know,

I have been living here for many years,

and I have come to understand

that the blacks are just like us.

They can be fat they can be thin,

they can be big they can be small,

they can be poor, but also, they can be rich.]

JIMBO: But I wouldn't want to be a rich black person.

You know?

It wouldn't be . . . very authentic.

I'm just thinking critically about it and,

don't you think that once a person has enough money,

their race just kind of disappears and they're just rich?

Like, if I'm going to be black,

I'd want to be a normal black person,

to like have that experience,

of like going to da club, you know?

Gettin' rowdy.

MACK: Oh my god.

You'd just want to be black so you could say the N-word.

JIMBO: That's not what I meant.

MACK *(Sing-song)*: You wanna say the N-word.

You wanna say the N-word.

JIMBO: I mean, sure, I'd fucking say it if I were a black person.

I can say it now, if I want to.

I can say whatever the fuck I want, I don't give a fuck.

BETS: Who cares what you call her or her,

say what you want who cares?

In America you are obsessed with race,

and you never never never think about class.

The rich profit from the racism.

The poor get nothing from it.

JIMBO: [And that shit happens alla the time,
       you got to get yours before I got to get mine.]

BETS: But I'm not so interested in this, you know,
       ghetto-type of kind of thing.

JIMBO: Well, if you want to be a real black person,
       then you have to be a poor black person.

MACK: No that's more of a gender question than a class question.
       Like maybe you'd have to be poor
       if you wanted to be a black man,
       but if you wanted to be a black woman, you could be like . . .
       a fabulous entertainer.
       Like, that would be amazing, to be like:
       Hair! Body! Voice!
       Like black women are . . . fierce.
       [I think there could be something really . . . empowering,
       being a black woman.]
       Like look at the way they talk to each other.

(Beat, they watch.)

There's just so much . . . attitude.

(Beat, they watch.)

I just love that. Do you see what I mean?

(Beat, they watch.)

BETS: I do. I do.

MACK: It's like . . . You can't tell me what to do!

(Beat, they watch.)

BETS: You don't know who I am!

(Beat, they watch.)

MACK: "I'm out here living my best life."
BETS: Oh, I like that.

(Keisha enters.
This text tethers directly with the text that was/is being delivered
by the family onstage.
For the most part:
Suze tethers with Keisha [starting with her clean and starving
dance].
Jimbo tethers with Jasmine [starting with her line "what's that."].
Mack tethers with Beverly [starting with her line ". . . the gown."].
Bets tethers with Dayton [starting with his line "Mama Frasier
Birthday dance!"].)

SUZE: Are you people insane?
  You have no idea what you're talking about.
  [You just— You don't. You just—]
  You don't, you have no idea what it would be like
  to be African-American.
  [That is not how African-American women speak, or think,
  or feel,]
  [and I can't—I can't even—I can't—I can't even—]
JIMBO: Why are you freaking out?
SUZE: I'm not freaking out, but you just have no idea what you're
  talking about.
JIMBO: You think you'd be a good black woman?
  That is hard for me to imagine,
  like can you imagine her being a black woman?
MACK: Not really.
JIMBO: Not at all.

MACK: Like, not at all.

JIMBO: If she was black
she would be like the most uptight black woman
that has ever existed.

MACK: Sorry, but you're not very cool.

JIMBO: She's the opposite of cool.

MACK: Like, the way you hold your body is just so . . .

JIMBO: She's so stiff.

MACK: [You are] Very rigid.

JIMBO: Like you're all in your head all the time,
and you don't know how to be chill.
Like most black people are really chill.

MACK: And they're really fashionable.

JIMBO: There's this way they dress, there's an attitude.

MACK: And like their hair, is always done.

JIMBO: There's a swagger, and a
and you're not like—

MACK: I reaaally wish I knew,
like how they diiiiid their hair.

JIMBO: Oh yeaaaah,
like when it's all like twiiiiisted up and stuff?

MACK: Yeah.

BETS: I just love it when they dance!
Like: Oooooh, the women.

MACK: I know! Ooooh, cha-cha-cha-cha.

BETS AND MACK: Ooooh, they can dance.
Yesss (Yaaaas), they love to dance.

BETS, MACK AND JIMBO: Yeess (Yaaas)(Yeeaah), black people sing.

SUZE: But—

BETS, MACK AND JIMBO: Yeess (Yaaas)(Yeeaah), black people dance.

SUZE: But—

BETS, MACK AND JIMBO: Yeess (Yaaas)(Yeeaah), black people love—

SUZE: But—

BETS, MACK AND JIMBO: —to siiiiing and dance around!

(With Keisha's aside.

*But here is a moment where Keisha, instead of delivering her
aside, might check her hair, outfit, teeth in the pretend mirror
hung on the fourth wall, and, then, she might be able to look
through it, and see the audience.)*

SUZE: But being black isn't just about singing and dancing
and . . . hair.
That's part of it, but that's not all of it.
This history of oppression and inequity, it is in everything.
Mabel loved me and I loved her, but there was always this—
membrane between us.
When we walked down the street,
I knew what people thought.
And it made me so self-conscious.
And that's really terrible.
Like if I could have just loved Mabel,
and had it not be like a Thing.
Not have this like external thing make that love . . .
make me ashamed of that feeling.
Like if I could just be my authentic feeling . . . that would be.
I think it would be amazing.

*(The tethering gets even closer now, almost syllable for syllable.
On the shift out of Keisha's aside and Dayton's line:)*

JIMBO: You'd be a terrible black woman.
SUZE: What are you talk[ing about]—
JIMBO: Terrible.
SUZE: Me?!
JIMBO: Yup.

(On Keisha's exit:)

SUZE: They would love me if they met me.

MACK: Hold up, are you a dancer?

BETS: Well,

MACK: Got those real dance moves.

BETS: well,

MACK: You a freak.

BETS: well.

MACK: Don't lie to me, I know you dance.

BETS: Yes.

MACK: I knew it, me too times a million,
    I love dance, I live dance, I dream dance.

BETS: Don't we all?

MACK: Alright.
    Bitches, this a Dance Party.

BETS: Yes!

MACK: Par-tay. Like it's nineteen ninety-nine.
    We have to.

SUZE: Have to do what, have like a dance party?

MACK: It is happening.

SUZE: Why would we have a dance party?

MACK: Why?

SUZE: I don't dance. Dancing . . . feels weird.

MACK: Mmm-hmmm.

SUZE: I'd rather talk . . . what?

MACK: Girlfriend, I can't even.
    Your little life is so tragic and introverted and repressed.

SUZE: Stop, I just don't dance.

MACK: You know you're sexually repressed if your hips don't
    move.

SUZE: I'm not repressed or like introverted.

MACK: Oh, you're sexually like a problem,
    yes that is clear all together,
    you better believe that.

SUZE: . . .

MACK: Now I know that you won't dance
   because you are afraid that you're bad at it,
   that people will see that you have no rhythm and think,
   "Oooh. That woman is bad at Sex."

SUZE: . . .

JIMBO: I dance like a boss and I can fuck all night.

MACK: This one doesn't need to be like a ho right now, ok.
   What this one needs to do is try to be in her body,
   and explore her sexual consciousness,
   and let her Body take control.
   That's what this one needs to do.

SUZE: Just stop.

MACK: And then you'll realize dancing helps you
   to keep on getting laid.

JIMBO: And if you like doing black things you might be—

MACK: That is not what I'm talking about ok,
   I am saying that dancing—

BETS: That dancing is sensual and fun—

MACK: If you don't love your body, who's gonna love it? Hmmn?
   Truth.

BETS: Let sex move round the hips.

JIMBO: Seriously, why does dancing feel like so damn good?

MACK: I know.

BETS: Can we start to dance now?

JIMBO: Want to hear my moves?*(Does a little beatbox-type sound)*

MACK: *(Gasp)*

JIMBO: Fo' sho.

MACK: Niiiiiiice.

BETS: But for the music—

JIMBO: Dancing like without a beat is like,

MACK: I have a mix,

JIMBO: not even dancing.

MACK: a like dance mix.

BETS: I will put on the radio.

MACK: I have a mix.

JIMBO: Why don't you play your mix and we'll get this started.

MACK: Wait wait wait wait wait—

She's going to faint now.

BETS: Is she?

MACK: I think so . . .

(Beverly faints, spilling carrots all over the floor.
Jasmine and Dayton gasp in horror.)

(Cackling) The carrots!

(Keisha runs in.)

Mama? Mama!

(And the actions onstage continue, as described on page 75. ***)

SUZE: Is she ok?

JIMBO: Of course she's ok.

MACK: She's fine. Look, she's like,

Oh my god, I can't believe I ruined my beautiful dinner.

BETS: The dinner is not so beautiful.

SUZE: It's lovely.

BETS: And these horrible chairs, so bizarre.

SUZE: There's nothing wrong with them.

MACK: I'd never noticed them.

BETS: They have no taste, this family.

MACK: They are a little—

JIMBO: And her, with the wine.

SUZE: Keisha seems so upset.

JIMBO: I bet she is.

SUZE: What is that supposed to mean.

JIMBO: No, just that she's—

MACK: He's so possessive of her.

BETS: Who?

MACK: Dayton.

BETS: Is he?

MACK: He's like, Don't give wine to my woman.

That's controlling, isn't it?

BETS: I hadn't noticed that.

SUZE: She Just fainted.

(Keisha exits.)

JIMBO: Where's she running to, Beverly?

MACK: I bet she's going to call Erika?

BETS: Who is Erika?

[MACK: Her Friend from School.]

[BETS: I don't understand.]

JIMBO: Yeah, who is Erika?

MACK: Keisha's Friend from School. Oh my god.

SUZE: She was just getting the cake out of the oven.

MACK: You have no idea what it is like to be a teenage girl.

BETS: Why did they burn the cake?

MACK: That cake is on fire, honey.

SUZE: It wasn't on purpose.

JIMBO: It's a cakewalk!

SUZE: Shut up.

JIMBO: It is.

SUZE: Shut up.

You are the worst.

(Dayton talks to Beverly.)

JIMBO: Wait, and I love this, he's like:

MACK: What?

(Jimbo performs a line from the spoken intro or an interlude of a R&B song.)

BETS: I don't know this song.

(Mack performs some background vocals, or an instrumental part of the same song.)

No. I don't know it.

(Jimbo and Mack sing part of the song's chorus.)

No, I still, I don't know it.

MACK: Really?

BETS: No.

MACK: You'd love it.

BETS: Why.

MACK: Because it's . . . well. People like.

People like, like to fuck to it.

BETS: Oh!

MACK: Yeah.

BETS: Can we hear it?

MACK: Of course.

SUZE: Can we not?

BETS: What is your problem?

(Dayton exits.)

JIMBO: And where's he gone now, Beverly?

SUZE: To buy a cake.

JIMBO: I don't think so.

SUZE: For the grandmother's birthday. Obviously.

JIMBO: Why are you being so prissy.

SUZE: Prissy?!

JIMBO: You're a prissy little girl,

SUZE: Little Girl?

JIMBO: and, if you think you could be a black woman,
    you need to be able to be a fucking man, and like, step up.

SUZE: What.

JIMBO: Like you should be like I'm going to be black,
and if someone has something to say about it,
then, like, step up.

SUZE: What does step up . . . sorry, what does step up mean?

JIMBO: What do you mean.

It means step up.

SUZE: Step up on what?

JIMBO: Step up.

SUZE: Step up to what?

JIMBO: Just like, step up.

SUZE: For what?

JIMBO: I can't tell you how to step up. You just step up.

(Jasmine shouts:)

BETS: Fine, Mama! Fine! I will run off with Antoine.

MACK: Um . . . What?

BETS: He play the sax and he love me!

She would say something like that, I think.

MACK: Well, she is fabulous.

BETS: She's the interesting one. The one with romance.

MACK: She's the best-dressed one, I think.

BETS: Oh, I agree.

Oh, oops!

MACK: She's like, I'm not drunk, I didn't even spill my wine.

BETS: She? Spill wine?

MACK: Of course not.

BETS: I love that. She wrings the most from this little life she has.

Oh no. Why is she taking the things from the table?

SUZE: She's not stealing them.

BETS: I didn't say she was stealing.

MACK: She is not made for housework.

BETS: Is she leaving?

MACK: Oh no.

BETS: Where is she going?

JIMBO: Where's she gone to, Beverly?

SUZE: Will you stop saying that?

BETS: I hate it when she leaves.

It is so boring when she is gone.

SUZE: What are you talking about.

MACK: I know. These two are like, blech, so boring.

SUZE: They are the heart and the soul of the whole—

BETS: I like the grandmother best.

She has some glamour around her.

SUZE: The grandmother is the heart and the soul of the whole family [in the African-American tradition]—

BETS: She's back!

MACK: Welcome back!

BETS: Yay!

MACK: Get yourself a drink, girl!

BETS: Fill it up!

MACK: Let's get our drink on!

JIMBO: And our smoke on! And go home with,

BETS: And put on some jazz!

(Jasmine turns music on.)

SUZE: What?

MACK: Sorry, No.

JIMBO: I hate jazz.

BETS: Have you ever been to the festival at Montreux?

MACK: No.

BETS: Really? You should. It's very good.

Very good jazz.

Now, to sing jazz, that is a good reason to be a black.

SUZE: You have no idea what you are talking about.

BETS: I might want to be a black.

SUZE: Well, you don't.

BETS: People say I have a black woman inside of me.

SUZE: You don't.

MACK: I'm not even listening to you guys anymore.
I'm just watching them dance.

BETS: Yes, we are missing the dancing.

JIMBO: I'm not missing a fucking thing.

BETS: I would love to dance like this
With you know—

MACK: With hips and shoulders.

BETS: Yes, hips and shoulders.
It is hard to say.
Hips and—

MACK: Shoulders.

BETS: Shoulders?

MACK: Yes, shoulders.

JIMBO: I don't trust that one.

MACK: Which one.

JIMBO: That one.
It's like she's working too hard to seem nice, you know.

BETS: Oh thank god they cover the table.

SUZE: There's nothing wrong with the table.

BETS: There is something wrong with all of this.

(Dayton enters with a cake.)

JIMBO: It's another cakewalk!

SUZE: Jesus Christ.

MACK: And what Is a cakewalk anyway?

SUZE: It's racist.

MACK: I know that. But what *is* it.

BETS: Why is it racist?

SUZE: It's a racist dance
where black people pretend they have easy lives.

JIMBO: That's not what a cakewalk is.

BETS: But they burn the cake.

SUZE: It's a racist dance
  where black people pretend to have easy lives,
  so we don't feel bad about how bad their lives actually are.

JIMBO: A cakewalk is just when black people pretend to be rich
  white people.

MACK: But that sounds . . . why is that racist?

JIMBO: It's not, actually.

SUZE: Yes it is.

JIMBO: It's just that we think that everything black people had to
  do back in the day is racist now.

SUZE: That is because everything was racist back in the day.

JIMBO: No, everything is racist now, which means that nothing
  is racist now.

BETS: I am not racist.

SUZE: Yes, you kind of are.

BETS: I am not.

MACK: She is not.

SUZE: Everyone is racist.

JIMBO: It's like if everything is racist,
  that means that nothing is racist.

BETS: I am not a racist. You do not say this to me.

JIMBO: It's like this movie.

SUZE: I'm saying that I am racist too, ok, it's not just you.

MACK: I don't even understand what point you're trying to make.

JIMBO: No, but it's like this movie.

SUZE: No, just that race is a construct, but it's a very—

JIMBO: WILL YOU ALL JUST SHUT THE FUCK UP
  AND LISTEN TO ME?
  I'M TRYING TO MAKE A FUCKING POINT. GODDAMN.
  (The family dances and sets the table)
  Because like, did you guys see the movie
  where these college kids go abroad and—
  The movie—it's a series.

And in the first one, the college kids,
they go abroad to like, Europe.
They're like doing that
with the backpack
and like drinking and weed and hanging out and you know
they meet some girls real cute and blond
and it turns out the girls are like
friends with these crazy rich people.
Or maybe the girls Are the crazy rich people?
I don't remember but somebody's homicidal and super rich
and so the college kids are in this foreign prison.
And it is filled with rich people that have like
these like killing-people fetishes and
fucking-people-up fetishes
like really weird stuff and everything's all brown and bloody
and everyone is dirty and screaming
and the college kids are all crying and scared
because they hadn't been anywhere like that before.
Shitting themselves, you know.
Of course they're scared.
But it's weird because,
because nobody thinks about how all the crazy rich people
got into that, you know?
You don't just have a whole hobby about torturing people
on accident.
You don't just fall into that shit casually, you know.
Like, you don't build your whole life around brutality
by mistake.
You have to want that.
You have to plan that.
And people don't think about that.
But I think about that.
My mind works different.
And in the movie, the college kids are sold

to the crazy rich people
and the rich people kill them
in like intense and brutal ways.
And, That's basically the movie.
And it's like Awesome.
Like one of the rich crazy people has this fetish
that is like cutting people's fingers off with chainsaws
or some shit
and so he's doing that with the chainsaw
vrrr-ng-ng-ng-ng
and slips in blood or something
and the rich guy decapitates himself
with his own chainsaw.
And it's obvious what that means.
Do you know what I mean?
It means he's the victim of his own damn thing.
Like he's the victim of his own shit,
like, we're all the victim of our own shit, right?
Like, Of course he is.
And it always happens, it's always like that.
Like that just keeps happening in different ways
in the whole series,
and that's why they're all like a little bit actually good,
you know?
Yeah, like there's a good moral thing going on,
like educating people,
and being like
whatever the fuck you come up with to do to somebody else
it always ends up getting used on you.
And that shit is moral you know?
You know what I'm saying?
He's the victim of his own fucking fetish.
And it's like. I'm not some mindless fucking person,
like I can't just do something, I've got to think about it.
You know I can't just listen to something I have to hear it

you know.
And make it.
Like I make a movie in my mind of what I do every day.
You know?
I make a movie in my mind of what I do every single day.
Like I hear my music underneath me.
And I know my function in it.
Like I'm not just doing what I'm doing
I know what I'm doing, you know what I mean?
Like I can see it clear as fucking day,
the movie that I make in my head of what I'm doing,
like I am outside of my own body,
and I see myself, and my actions,
and I see how everybody fucking looks at me,
and I know what everybody fucking thinks about me.
Like they don't even realize how thoroughly I understand
every single fucking thought in all their heads.
Like I'm making the movie, motherfucker,
I know what you're fucking thinking
and I know what you're fucking seeing,
because I am in control of all of it.
Of all of it.
So it's like, yeah, I know
I fucking know
I know that I'm not the hero of my movie.
I'm making the motherfucking movie,
this is my fucking movie
so I understand that I'm not the hero of my movie,
I am fucking aware.
I am fucking aware.
And I keep making the movie,
and I root against myself,
and I keep making the movie,
and I keep being victorious,
and I keep winning everything,

I win everything,
and I keep winning Because I'm the villain of this movie,
motherfuckers
do you see what I mean,
like, fuck yeah I'm the villain
and I'm bigger and meaner and faster and I fucking own that
and I'm fucking owning that every day
and I'm smarter and richer and I fucking dominate
that's who the fuck I am
that's who the fuck I am
and it's like I love to root against myself
because every fucking person is rooting against me too
like every other . . .
yeah, every other fucking thing
every other fucking person, or race, or whatever the fuck,
every other thing, they're all rooting against me,
all of them are rooting against me,
and I fucking Know that shit,
I know that
and I love it
I fucking love it
because you know what?
All those motherfuckers are watching my fucking movie.
And rooting for whatever the fuck they want
in my fucking movie.
Like, you want to make me the villain?
That's fine because you're in my fucking movie
motherfucker.
And it's a good fucking movie.
Like, my movie is dope as shit and fucking deep.
All these motherfuckers in my movie know
what the fuck is up.
They need me to be the villain.
Do you know what I mean?
They fucking need me to.

They're fucking gagging for it.
All these fucking people,
they wouldn't know what the fuck to do
if they couldn't root against me.
They'd be fucking lost without me,
do you know what I mean?
Hey.
Do you know what I mean?
HEY.
I'M TALKING TO YOU FUCKERS.
DO YOU KNOW WHAT I FUCKING MEAN????!!

END OF TEXT OF ACT TWO

*** *The actions onstage continue after Beverly faints Like . . . ok . . .*
something like:
Keisha runs over to Beverly.
Beverly says she's fine.
*Keisha and Dayton help Beverly off the floor, while she's insisting
that she's fine.*
*Jasmine pours a glass of wine for Beverly . . . and a glass of wine for
herself.*
Jasmine brings wine over to Beverly.
*Dayton gives her a look and asks Jasmine to get Beverly a glass of
water.*
*Jasmine gives Dayton a look and says that she knows what's best for
her sister.*
*Keisha remembers that the burning cake is still in the oven, and runs
into the kitchen.*
Dayton says he knows what's best for his wife.
Jasmine and Dayton start to argue, and Beverly asks for water.

Jasmine and Dayton both say I'll get it and start toward the kitchen.
Keisha comes bursting out of the kitchen holding a smoking cake pan
with oven mitts.
All wave away the smoke.
Jasmine goes to the kitchen to get Beverly a glass of water.
Beverly takes Dayton's hand and tells him that she loves him,
and that she just wants the day to go well.
Dayton comforts Beverly and he says a monologue that is something
like: "Did I ever tell you about my ninth birthday party? Well, it was
supposed to be great and my dad had planned it all perfectly, and
I was so excited, but then no one I invited came, and so it was just
me and my dad eating birthday cake, and it was the best birthday
I ever had."
Beverly and Dayton have a moment, it's sweet.
Jasmine enters with a glass of water and is like do you want it or not.
Keisha enters: like Dad you need to get a cake.
Beverly takes the water and takes a sip.
Dayton grabs his wallet and car keys and goes out to buy a cake.
Beverly goes over and starts picking carrots up off the floor,
and asks Jasmine to help.
Jasmine looks at her outfit and is like I'm not getting on the floor in
this.
Keisha goes to help.
Beverly feels a little woozy.
Keisha is like, Mom, you just fainted, I've got it.
Jasmine leads Beverly over to sit and gives her a glass of wine,
and pours herself another glass.
Beverly asks Jasmine if she's had enough wine.
Jasmine says that she's fine, and says something about their mother.
Beverly is like our mother can hear you.
Jasmine is like good! and repeats what she said shouting up the stairs
so Mama can hear it.
Beverly is like don't even start with her, you're drunk.
Jasmine is like I am not drunk and trips.
Beverly is like, omg are you ok?

Jasmine is like look, I didn't even spill my wine, I'm fine.

Keisha is like, omg, you guys are crazy, what should I do with these carrots I've picked up.

Jasmine is like I know what to do with them, and is like hold my wine, and she takes the carrots, cutting board and whatever else out the front door.

Keisha is like Jasmine is cray and Beverly is like Jasmine is cray and Jasmine comes back in dusting off her hands and is like, work is done for the day, I thought this was supposed to be a party.

Beverly is like, did you just throw my cutting board on my front lawn?

And Jasmine is like, YUP, and turns on some music.

And Beverly is like I can't believe I have to go out and get my cutting board, oh, And my knife.

And Jasmine is like leave it, it'll be there tomorrow.

And Beverly recognizes the song, and is like I love this song, but also Jasmine you are crazy and I'm still mad at you.

And Jasmine is like you love me, we're sisters.

And Keisha is like, oh now I know what song this is!

And they all do a dance to it, like an electric slide–type dance.

And Keisha is like I dance so much better than you old ladies.

And Beverly is like, who are you calling old, I can get down, uh uh uh.

And Jasmine is like I didn't know you still had it in you.

And Beverly is like, yeah, putting it down, uh uh uh.

And Jasmine is like yeah, uh uh uh.

And Keisha is like double time uh-uh uh-uh uh-uh.

And Dayton comes in with car keys and cake from the store and is like he-ey it's a partay.

And Beverly is like at least put the cake down.

And Dayton is like oh I can dance with this cake and does like the roger rabbit or something while holding the cake.

And everyone's like whooo!

And everyone goes back into the electric slide–type dance.

And they dance all over the space,

and start to get the table set for dinner.

In some order, and with lots of other things happening:

They dance and set the table.
Jasmine pours Keisha some wine,
and Beverly takes the wine away from Keisha.
They dance and get the centerpiece and candles.
Jasmine moves the centerpiece
and Beverly moves it back
and Jasmine moves it again
and Beverly moves it back again.
They dance and put out plates of fake food and bowls of fake food,
and Dayton dances over to the TV and dances while watching the
big game.
And Beverly dances the remote control away from him
and he dances back into the kitchen to help,
and they dance and put out a whole other set of plates of food and
bowls of food,
dancing so Joyfully and so Well,
and the fake foods get stranger and stranger,
in different ways, some of it is faker and some of it is less food-like,
and the family brings it all out of the kitchen while dancing,
and smiling, with glee,
and puts it on the table, piling it up,
maybe till it threatens to overflow the table,
and maybe at one point there is a conga line of fake food
and it's so fun and joyful,
and eventually they're finally done bringing out food
so they dance themselves to their seats, grinning,
and they dance-applaud Beverly for making this beautiful meal,
and Beverly dance-accepts,
and then they all sit down at the table for dinner,
and Beverly gets ready to call up the stairs for Mama.

END OF ACTION OF ACT TWO

ACT THREE

BEVERLY: Mama?

Mama? Can you come down here please?

We're ready for you.

(A new song starts. Entrance music for a good-hearted black grandma.

"Mama" comes to the top of the stairs.

It is Suze, one of the women who has been listening.

She's wearing something like an ivory gown with golden threads.

And on her head, something like a golden turban

with a rhinestone at the center.

All look at her.

She looks at them.

She Descends The Staircase.

She has a Moment.

And at an appropriate moment in the music,

the volume dips down for Beverly's line:)

Oh, Mama, you look beautiful.

Doesn't she look Beautiful, Jasmine?

JASMINE: Oh, yes. Just gorgeous.

BEVERLY: Do you think you might give us a little dance today, Mama?

DAYTON: Let the woman be.

BEVERLY: I'm not bothering her.

JASMINE: Happy birthday, Mama.

BEVERLY: Should we say grace? Let's join hands.

Keisha, take your grandmother's hand, what's the matter with you.

(Keisha does.
Beverly, Jasmine and Dayton bow their heads.
Keisha looks at Suze.
Suze beams. She looks at all of them, and at us;
she can't help it, she's just so happy to be here.)

Thank you, heavenly father, for bringing us together,

for giving us all that we have,

for hearing our pain and hearing our joy

and guiding us through our lives

as best you can, dear lord.

[Thank you for the roof over our heads,

for the floor under our feet.]

Thank you for watching over us,

for listening to our prayers,

for hearing our fears,

for guiding us in accordance with your divine plan.

Thank you, heavenly father, for giving us this food,

that will nourish our bodies, just as you nourish our souls.

Amen.

DAYTON AND JASMINE: Amen.

BEVERLY: Alright, let's eat!

DAYTON: This all looks amazing, Bev.

(Jasmine and Dayton start serving themselves. Beverly hovers nervously.)

BEVERLY: Thank you Dayton.

DAYTON: You've outdone yourself. Don't you think so, Jasmine?

JASMINE: Well, I haven't tasted it yet.

BEVERLY: Mama, do you want me to fix you a plate?

(Suze looks at her.)

Alright, then. I'll get all your favorites.
Keisha, what's the matter.

JASMINE: Why aren't you eating baby?

KEISHA: It's not . . . Um. I'm just confused. I guess.

JASMINE: What's the matter Keisha?

KEISHA: I'm just a little out of it. I—

BEVERLY: Drink some water.

KEISHA: Yeah. I'm gonna just sit down for a second.

JASMINE: You are sitting down.

KEISHA: Yeah. Just a second.

JASMINE: What's the matter with her?

BEVERLY: I don't know. Teenagers.

(Keisha sits on the floor and watches Suze.)

Is this enough food for you Mama?
Dayton, do you think this is enough?

DAYTON: It's fine, Beverly.

BEVERLY: Okay, here you go. Do you want me to cut it up for you, Mama?

DAYTON: She can do it, can't you Mama Frasier?
Just let her be, Bev.

BEVERLY: You're right. Sorry Mama. Ok everybody, let's eat.

(They pretend to eat.)

DAYTON: Mmmm, mmmm, MMMM! Dang, Bev!
You outdone yourself this year, boy.

BEVERLY: Is it alright?

DAYTON: It's delicious, isn't it Jasmine.

BEVERLY: I was worried that the potatoes would be too salty.

JASMINE: They are a little salty.

DAYTON: Well, I like 'em.

JASMINE: They're very tasty.

DAYTON: Delicious!

JASMINE: When you get a bite of something
less Flavorful with them, it all balances out.

BEVERLY: What do you think, Mama?

DAYTON: Mmmm, Mmmm, Mmmm. Good.

BEVERLY: Dayton, you're going to choke.

JASMINE: Can you stop worrying over everybody?

DAYTON: She has a point Bev, you gotta relax.

JASMINE: If you don't relax, how's anybody supposed to even try
to enjoy this flavorful food you've prepared?

DAYTON: Take it easy, Bev.
Let's all just take a minute and calm down and eat.

(They all pretend to eat.
Keisha has an aside:)

KEISHA: I just feel like something is wrong.
I have a pit in my stomach and my heart is—

SUZE *(To Keisha, aside)*: I felt the same way when I was your age.

(Keisha jumps up, startled, because Suze has entered her aside.)

I was your age once.

KEISHA: What—what—

SUZE: Oh, Keisha, I understand you, more than you realize.
I've known you since you were born.

KEISHA: *(Glares)*

SUZE: Alright. That's alright.

But you can talk to me. I'm here to listen.

(Suze makes a vague hand gesture, like a conductor.
The music comes back on.
The conversation picks up where they left off.)

JASMINE: I'm telling you, if you load up your fork,
you get a bit of that salty food on there
with the food that isn't seasoned,
and it all balances out.

BEVERLY: Come over here and get a plate Keisha.
I thought you were hungry.

DAYTON: Let the child alone, Bev.

JASMINE: Is there any butter in the potatoes?

BEVERLY: Oh. There is.

JASMINE: Well, that's dairy, isn't it?

BEVERLY: Yes. It is.

(Their eyes meet—a showdown. Jasmine relents.)

JASMINE: I just wish I'd known.

(Beat.
A doorbell ring sound.)

DAYTON: Keisha, will you get the door.

(Beat.)

BEVERLY: Keisha?

JASMINE: I'll get it.

BEVERLY: Keisha, what's the matter?

KEISHA: I'm fine.

DAYTON: Your mother needs you today Keisha.

(Jasmine enters.)

JASMINE: It's Tyrone. He made it after all.

(Jimbo makes an entrance with music, stunting.
He's probably wearing a baseball cap and some sneakers.
Maybe a chain.
He raps along to his entrance music for us and the family, and
he might try to get the crowd on their feet. The whole entrance
should probably end with a bad-ass pose.)

JIMBO: How you doin' Mama?
    Sorry I'm late, y'all.
JASMINE: It's not a problem.
DAYTON: Hey there Tyrone.

(Jimbo dabs.)

    Yup, alright.
JASMINE: We're all so glad you're here.
BEVERLY: We didn't wait for you to start,
    since I didn't know if you would make it.
JIMBO: Well, I did.
BEVERLY: Yes, you did.
DAYTON: Beverly.
JASMINE: You must be so tired from your flight.
JIMBO: I'm fuckin' spent.
SUZE: Tyrone. Language.
JIMBO: Sorry. Mama.
    What's up with Keisha?
BEVERLY: She's just resting for a moment.
    I don't think she's feeling well.
JIMBO: I bet she ain't.
BEVERLY: What is that supposed to mean?
JIMBO: How you doin' Keisha?

JASMINE: Keisha, your uncle said something to you.

JIMBO: What's the matter Keisha?

SUZE: Leave Keisha alone.

DAYTON: Can I get you a glass of wine, Tyrone?

JIMBO: Let me get a beer.

BEVERLY: With dinner?

DAYTON: Oh, sure, I think we have a few in the fridge, don't we Beverly?

BEVERLY: I'll check.

JIMBO: Dope dope dope.

(Beverly exits.)

JASMINE: So, Tyrone. How is work?

JIMBO: What?

JASMINE: Do you think you're going to make partner?

JIMBO: I don't know.

Why isn't there music on?

Isn't there supposed to be music on?

SUZE: That's enough, Tyrone.

JIMBO: Come on! I want to dance! Five, six, seven, eight:

(Upbeat music comes on.
Jimbo starts dancing.
Jimbo gets Suze up and dancing.
Somehow they know the same dance.
They do that thing—like an exaggerated wave,
and Jasmine and Dayton jump up and join in.
Keisha marks it.
Beverly reenters with a bottle of beer,
and joins in while holding a beer.)

BEVERLY: What's all this?

JIMBO: We Frasiers love to dance.

DAYTON: You Frasiers do love to dance.

JASMINE: We Frasiers love to dance.
BEVERLY: We Frasiers love to dance.
JIMBO: No no no. This isn't the kind of beer you'd have.
BEVERLY: What do you mean, Tyrone?
JIMBO: Don't you have like . . . I don't know
a forty or something. Like a Colt 45?
BEVERLY: . . . I'll check.

(Beverly exits.)

JIMBO: This is fun.

(A doorbell ring sound.)

I bet it's that girl from Keisha's school.
SUZE: Alright now, Tyrone.
JASMINE: What girl?
SUZE: Maybe you don't need that beer.
DAYTON: I'll get it.

(The music shifts to Mack's entrance music.
The dancing shifts accordingly.
Mack enters, choreographed within an inch of all of our lives.
There might be a costume reveal. There is at least one wig reveal.
There might be a death drop.
Mack is dressed like a drag version of a black teenage girl.
Think glitter. Think sequins. Think confetti.
Mack lip-synchs, vogues, and flirts until
there is maybe a final pose, and hold for applause . . .)

MACK *(To Suze and Jimbo)*: Was that too much?
I didn't want her to be boring.
JIMBO: No, that was dope.
MACK: Thank you.
SUZE: You guys are ruining everything.

MACK: Oh my god, relax.
(To all:)
I am Erika!
Haaay!
Fabulous? Obviously.
Adorable? Of course.
A bad bitch? The baddest.
Do I feel naughty? I do.
Are we loving it? We are.
Am I here for Keisha? Absolutely.
Hey girl.

(Beverly enters with a forty of Colt 45.)

BEVERLY: Oh. Hello Erika.
MACK: Hello Beverly.
DAYTON: Erika, do you want to stay for dinner?
MACK: I wouldn't want to intrude!
BEVERLY: Well, thanks for stopping by—
MACK: I wouldn't want to impose!
JASMINE: Mama, you don't mind if Erika stays, do you?
SUZE: Me?
JASMINE: It's your party, Mama.
MACK *(To Keisha)*: I have what you asked for.
KEISHA: . . .
MACK: You know. The, um, assignment.
KEISHA: . . .
MACK: That you told your family that we talked about
on the phone.

(He presents an envelope.)

KEISHA: I didn't ask for anything.
JIMBO: Beverly, what is that now?

(Beverly takes the envelope.)

KEISHA: Mom!

MACK: That is for Keisha!

JIMBO: What is going on with your daughter?

BEVERLY: What kind of assignment is this?

JIMBO: Aw sheet.

JASMINE: Don't ask her, open it.

KEISHA: Aunt Jasmine.

BEVERLY: Don't start Jasmine.

JASMINE: I'm not starting anything.

DAYTON: This is ridiculous. Give it here.

JIMBO: Open it, Damon.

SUZE: Dayton.

JIMBO: Right.

JASMINE: What is it?

DAYTON: It's—it's—

MACK: No! Don't say it.

Keisha, I didn't want it to come out this way.

JIMBO: It's a pregnancy test!

KEISHA: What?

MACK: What?

BEVERLY: What?

SUZE: No!

DAYTON: What do you need that for Keisha?

KEISHA: I don't—I don't—I don't—

JIMBO: Oh, Keisha.

MACK: It is a love letter!

JIMBO: It is a pregnancy test!

(It is a pregnancy test.)

MACK: Fine.

JASMINE: Oh my lord.

BEVERLY: Keisha. Baby. Are you pregnant?

KEISHA: Mom, no.

DAYTON: Keisha.

KEISHA: It's like literally I don't—

JIMBO: Whose baby is it?

KEISHA: I am not pregnant.

MACK: Oh, Keisha.

KEISHA: I'm just— I'm not pregnant.

JASMINE: But how do you know?

KEISHA: Because I'm not—there's no— I don't understand what's happening right now.

MACK: Because she and I—

BEVERLY: I'm so disappointed in you.

KEISHA: But I'm not—

MACK: Because she and I are—

SUZE: Oh, Keisha, just tell your mother and I what happened. We'll forgive you.

MACK: You are ruining everything.

JASMINE: You better take that test, Keisha.

KEISHA: But I'm not pregnant.

DAYTON: Can't you see that your mother is hurting?

JASMINE: You better go on up to the bathroom and take that test.

KEISHA: But—

JASMINE: If you ain't done nothing wrong, then you don't have anything to worry about.

(Keisha shuts her mouth, takes the test, exits.)

Mmmn.

BEVERLY: I don't believe it.

JASMINE: Mmmn mmmn mmmn.

BEVERLY: I just can't believe it.

JASMINE: Mmmn mmmn mmmn mmmn mmmn.

JIMBO: It is what it is.

Babies having babies.

MACK: Grandma Frasier is going to have something to say about this.

SUZE: I love Keisha unconditionally.

MACK: Not you. Her Grandma Frasier.

(A sultry jazz version of Suze's Grandma's entrance music plays.
Another Mama surrounded by haze at the top of the stairs.
A bigger, golder turban.
A bigger, golder everythang.
It is Bets, with a cigarette.
She is très sexy.
She slithers, then poses, then slithers, then poses,
enjoying the dance and the spotlight, turning the house into a
jazz club.)

SUZE: What the fuck.
JIMBO: Language.
SUZE: Shut up.
MACK: She's fabulous.
BETS: I am!
     Hello everyone!
SUZE: And what are you doing?
BETS: Living!
SUZE: Mmmn.
BETS: Loving!
SUZE: Mmmn.
BETS: Out Loud!
MACK: I love it.
BETS: Living, how do you say . . . my best life?
MACK: Qween.
BETS: Can I tell you something?
     I want to tell you something.
     Can I say it in a special light?
SUZE: No!

(A special light.)

BETS: Thank you.

Yes.

As the black woman, the world tell me: shhh.

Don't be so proud.

Don't be so sexy.

MACK: *(Snaps)*

BETS: The world tell me that I am too much.

Too loud.

Too aggressive.

Always.

Too sassy.

Always.

They fear me because I feel too much. I think too much.

But you know what?

MACK: You tell 'em, honey.

BETS: I am too much.

(Keisha reenters.)

KEISHA: Who is she?

BETS: I am your grandmother.

KEISHA: But—

BETS: Shall we do a little dance?

(Bets and Mack start Mama Frasier's birthday dance.)

JIMBO: No, we're past all that.

BETS: But—

JIMBO: What does the test say?

KEISHA: I don't want to say because everyone's going to freak out.

JASMINE: Oh my lord.

KEISHA: I'm not pregnant.

JIMBO: It's positive.

KEISHA: Yes, but I'm not pregnant.

BEVERLY: Let me see that.

BETS AND SUZE *(In unison)*: You better let your mama see it.

Stop it.

This is my—

Stop it.

Stop.

JASMINE: Let me see the damn test.

BEVERLY: What does it say.

JASMINE: It's—it's—

JIMBO: It's positive. Like I said.

BEVERLY: Oh my lord.

DAYTON: Let me see that.

KEISHA: Dad—it's not.

DAYTON: My little girl.

KEISHA: Daddy I'm not pregnant!

I can't be. Erika and I are—

MACK: Right! I thought we were—

KEISHA: Get away from me.

MACK: You're so cruel.

BEVERLY: You lie to me.

KEISHA: Mom.

BEVERLY: You running around doing who knows what
with who knows who—

KEISHA: Mom, I'm not—

BEVERLY: Stop it Keisha. Just stop.

JIMBO *(Sotto voce)*: Shit's about to get real.

BEVERLY: Coming in my house
sitting at my table
eating my food
looking me straight in my face
and lying to me.

KEISHA: Mom—

BEVERLY: And I couldn't see it because you're my daughter and
I love you,
but the scales have fallen from my eyes,

MACK *(Sotto voce)*: Mmn-hmm.

BEVERLY: and now I don't even recognize you.

MACK *(Sotto voce)*: Poof, be gone.

BEVERLY: You are not the daughter I raised.

KEISHA: No I am, Mom. I'm—

BEVERLY: My daughter wouldn't throw her whole future away.

My daughter would go to college, get an education.

SUZE *(Sotto voce)*: Poor Keisha.

KEISHA: I'm going to college.

JIMBO: Then whatchu gonna do with your baby, Keisha?

SUZE: I'll take care of the baby.

JASMINE: You've already raised your family, Mama.

BETS: My children have grown! It is my time to shine!

JASMINE: You've earned your rest.

BETS: I want to sing jazz!

SUZE: No, Jasmine, talk to me.

BETS: You are boring.

SUZE: I'm not boring. I just want . . .

(She attempts a beleaguered mammy/maid voice)

I wanna take care of the baby.

KEISHA: There is No Baby.

I am going to go to college.

I just want to find myself before I go—

(Jimbo takes out a stack of bills and eviction notices.)

JIMBO: There ain't no money for college, Keisha.

BEVERLY, JASMINE, DAYTON, MACK, SUZE AND BETS: What?

JIMBO: That dream is dead. Dead!

KEISHA: What are you talking about.

DAYTON: What's that you've got there?

JIMBO: Don't pretend like you don't know.

BETS: What has Dayton done now?

MACK: You know Uncle Tyrone got that tea.

(Jimbo hands the bills to Dayton.)

DAYTON *(Reading the bills)*: Past due. Past due.
BEVERLY: What?!
JASMINE: Oh my goodness.
DAYTON: I don't understand this.
BEVERLY: But I've seen you make the payments,
　　the mortgage payments,
　　every month.
DAYTON: I pay my bills.
JASMINE: Where's the money gone, Dayton?
SUZE: We're not losing the house, are we?
DAYTON: We are not losing the house.
JASMINE: Dayton, where's the money gone?
DAYTON: I don't know!
SUZE: We started off with nothing.
　　Worked for everything we had.
　　I worked my fingers to the bone,
　　cleaning other people's houses,
BEVERLY: But you never—
SUZE: just so, one day, I could buy my own.
BEVERLY: You never worked as a maid, Mama.
SUZE: And just like that. It's gone.
BETS: What on earth was that?
JASMINE: Where did all the money go?
JIMBO: Gambling.
ALL (OR MOST): *(Gasp!)*
JASMINE: No.
JIMBO: Yup.
JASMINE: Who?
BETS: Dayton.
ALL (OR MOST): *(Gasp!)*
DAYTON: What?
BETS: It must be.

JASMINE: Of course.

SUZE: No!

BETS: Yes.

JASMINE: When did it start?

MACK: What's gonna happen to Keisha?

SUZE: What have you done to this family?

BETS: What's going to happen to us all?

JASMINE: When did the gambling start?

DAYTON: It's not gambling, it's just fantasy football.
I don't understand this.

JASMINE: Then where did all the money go?

BETS: If it's not gambling, it's drugs.

ALL (OR MOST): Drugs?!

BETS: It's a common story.

SUZE: Who's on Drugs?

MACK: . . . Jasmine!

ALL (OR MOST): *(Gasp!)*

JASMINE: You better take my name outta your mouth, Erika.

MACK: Sorry, I don't know why I thought—it can't be Jasmine.

JIMBO: Is it . . . Beverly?

ALL (OR MOST): *(Gasp!)*

BEVERLY: Me?

JIMBO: I knew she was hiding something.

DAYTON: Oh, Beverly.

BEVERLY: I'm not—what drugs?

JASMINE: You have been acting funny.

BETS: She fainted!

SUZE: She's just tired.

JASMINE: She's been on edge, making mistakes,

BEVERLY: I have not!

JASMINE: She's been slipping.

SUZE: She's not on anything, is she?

BEVERLY: I'm not Mama.

DAYTON: This is serious Beverly.

JIMBO: Who been giving you drugs, Bea?

SUZE: She's a strong woman, trying to provide for her family, not some—

BETS: Crack woman!

SUZE: Please don't finish my sentences.

BEVERLY: Dayton, I don't know what this is all about.

DAYTON: Stop lying Beverly.

Just stop.

MACK *(Sotto voce)*: Ooooooh.

DAYTON: Have you been lying to me for so long?

So long that it just comes naturally to you?

JASMINE: Well it's not just her, Dayton, is it?

ALL (OR MOST): *(Gasp!)*

KEISHA: What?

JIMBO: Damn.

DAYTON: What are you talking about.

JASMINE: I knew it.

I just knew it.

Dayton is sick.

DAYTON: I'm not sick.

JASMINE: Lost the house, Beverly's on drugs, all this stress.

Come on now.

DAYTON: I'm not sick.

MACK: I think he is.

JASMINE: Oh I know he is.

MACK: What do you think he has.

JASMINE: Dayton what do you have?

MACK: Is it diabetes?

JASMINE: You got diabetes, Dayton?

MACK: Or worse!

JASMINE: Worse?

MACK: Like heart disease.

JASMINE: You gonna have a heart attack, Dayton?

MACK: Or, worse.

JASMINE: No!

MACK: Something venereal.

JASMINE: Oh my goodness!

MACK: Like syphilis.

JASMINE: You got syphilis, Dayton?!

DAYTON: Syphilis?!

SUZE AND BETS: Lord lord lord!

DAYTON: I don't have syphilis!

JASMINE: How could you.

MACK: Who have you been sleeping with, Dayton?

JIMBO: What?!

DAYTON: Beverly I haven't—

JASMINE: Don't you talk to her.

JIMBO: How dare you!

DAYTON: But I haven't—

BEVERLY: Why, Dayton, why?

JIMBO: How dare you cheat on my sister!

(Jimbo throws food at Dayton.
Dayton ducks and it hits Bets.)

Mama!

Mama I'm sorry—

BETS: What kind of a son throws food at his mother
on her birthday?

MACK: It's a food fight, bitches!

(FOOD FIGHT.
Jimbo, Mack, Bets and Suze are the aggressors,
for the most part.
Surprising things happen.
Some of it is silly, but eventually the silly gives way to violence
that feels more consequential.
Something is actually broken.
The set feels destroyed.)

KEISHA *(Aside)*: I need to ask you something.

SUZE *(Aside)*: Of course. Keisha. You can ask me anything.
You know that don't you.

KEISHA *(Aside)*: I know that you think you know what's best for
me—

SUZE *(Aside)*: I do, Keisha.

KEISHA *(Aside)*: But—

SUZE *(Aside)*: I've known you since the moment you were born.
I have watched you.
I brought you here and I watched you grow. Blossom.

KEISHA *(Aside)*: But—

SUZE *(Aside)*: Make beauty, out of . . . out of nothing,

KEISHA *(Aside)*: Please—

SUZE *(Aside)*: despite such hardship,
I'm so sorry that you've had to go thought that,
but I've watched you find such strength,
and I'm in awe of you and what you've accomplished,
I'm so proud of you and I am so happy for both of us,
for all I've done to make you who you are.
Oh, Keisha.
You don't know what it means to me.
To see this lovely girl who I have watched
for her entire life—

KEISHA *(Aside)*: No.
I have known You for My entire Life.

SUZE *(Aside)*: Keisha.

KEISHA: Stop.
Please, stop.

(Everything stops, or gets let go.
All listen to Keisha.)

I know what you're going to say because . . .
Because you have told me every story I have ever heard.

And I . . . I need you to listen.

Because I need to ask you something.

SUZE: Alright, Keisha. What do you want to ask me.

KEISHA: I . . .

I don't know.

I can't hear myself think.

I can't hear anything but you staring at me.

SUZE: I don't know what you're asking me to do Keisha.

KEISHA: I think I need to ask you . . . to not be here.

Or to let me not be here?

SUZE: You're not making sense. Maybe you should sit down.

KEISHA: I don't need to sit down.

I need to ask you to leave

so that I can have some space to think.

I can't think

in the face of you telling me who you think I am

with your loud self and your loud eyes

and your loud guilt—

I can't hear myself think.

SUZE: I don't know what I did to make you treat me this way.

All I've done, all I've ever done, is to try to be good to you.

KEISHA: Stop telling me that.

Stop telling yourself that.

Please. Just stop.

SUZE: You're not telling me what you want me to do Keisha.

KEISHA: I know. Because I don't know. I just want to . . .

I want to know what that space is.

What that space would be like.

For me.

Without.

Without you—

What should I call you.

SUZE: Hmmn. What would you want to call me?

KEISHA: Not Grandma.

(Beat.)

SUZE: That's. That's fair.

KEISHA: I'd call you.

Not Grandma.

I'd call you.

SUZE: You'd call me white.

KEISHA: I'd call you white. Yes.

Do you mind that?

SUZE: Why would I mind that?

KEISHA: I don't know.

SUZE: Do you want me to leave?

KEISHA: . . . no.

But do you think I could . . .

but what if I could . . .

SUZE: What if you could what?

KEISHA: What if we all could . . . what if we all could . . .

SUZE: Could what?

KEISHA: It would be too hard.

SUZE: We all could what?

KEISHA: And the same people who are always caught in between
would be caught in between.

SUZE: What if we all could do what?

KEISHA: Do you think I can ask them that anyway?

SUZE: Ask them what?

KEISHA: To switch?

SUZE: To switch what?

KEISHA: Do you think that I could—

What if I could?

But if I could ask the folks

who call themselves white

to come up here,

do you think they would?

Could I ask them to come up in here,

so that we could go down out there?
Do you think I could ask the folks
who call themselves white
to do that?
To switch for a little while?
How should I ask them, if I could?
Could I say,
Hi, white people.
Come here, white people. Come on up here.
If you're physically able to.

(Keisha steps through the fourth wall.
It's as simple as that.)

Could I say,
Come up here folks who identify as white,
you know who you are.
You can choose to come up here
to where I've always been, where my family has always been.
Sit on the couch.
Make yourself a plate.
Look out from where I am.
And let me and my family go out
to where you've always been.

Could I say that?
Could I ask them that?
How should I ask?
If I asked would they do it?
How long would it take?

Would it help if I told them that the show is ending?
Would it help white people to come up here
to where I've been
if I tell them that we'll all leave soon?

That there are things in motion already?
That we are all going to leave anyway?
Could I tell them that those seats are not theirs,
even though they paid for them?
That no one can own a seat forever?
That no one should?

Could I say,
See, there's Terri.
She's our stage manager.
She's amazing.
She's white.
She's coming up here.
You can come on up here too.
[Maybe you stand on the stage.
Maybe you stand near the stage.]
Leave your coats. Leave your bags. Leave your things.
Just stop worrying about your things, for a minute
and worry about where you can go
what you can do to make space for someone else
for a minute,
if you could.

Do I sound naive?
Does that matter?
Do I have to keep talking to them
and keep talking to them
and keep talking only to them
only to them
only to them
until I have used up every word
until I have nothing left for
You?

I've been trying to talk to You.
This whole time.

Have you heard me? [Thank you.]
Do I have to tell them that I want them to make space for us
for them to make space for us?
Do I really have to tell them that?
Do I have to tell them why I want them to go up there
for them to go up there?

Why I want them to sit on the sofa
and sit on the chairs
and sit on the carpet
and touch the walls
and touch the fake food
and touch your own face pretending to look in a mirror
but really looking into the lights?

They're bright aren't they?
Should I tell them that the lights are there
to help people see them,
not to help them see anything?
So I could be out down here with all my people of color?
With all my colorful people?
And we could be all of us together alone?
And if I were to be out here with my colorful people,
could I tell us a story?
If I were out here, just us, I'd want to tell us a story.
A story about ending.
Or about leaving.
Or about remaining.
And how they're all the same thing
if the same people do them.
But that's not the story I want to tell us all.
If I could tell the story I want to tell us,
my people,
my colorful people,
you would hear it

if I could tell it,
and it would be something like
a story about us, by us, for us, only us.
But that's not telling the story.

If I could tell the story I want to tell, it would begin like this:
Once upon a time, there was a bright little girl
who knew that if she worked twice as hard as—
No.
That's not what I wanted to tell.
Once, there was a little boy born with the deck stacked—
No.
Once, there was an exceptional—

It's difficult because I've already heard so many stories.
It's hard to find the one I'd wanted to tell.
It would be something like . . .

Once . . .
Well, not once,
not at all once.
Many many many many times,
there was a person who worked hard,
a person who tried to work hard,
and tried to do their best,
and tried to do well by their family,
and tried to be good, and tried to do better.
Many many times they tried this.
And so.
The person became who they always were—
who we all always are—
A Person Trying.

So they tried and they tried and they looked around
at the mountains of effort

that they had built with their trying
at the piles of half-built bests
at the heaps of family
at the hills of good enough hills and better next time,
and as they looked around,
as they took in the view,
they saw what they had done to make the life
that they had lived.

And they looked to the left and saw what you had done
to try to make the life that you have lived,
and they took in that view.

And they looked to the right and saw what you had done
to try to make the life that you have lived,
and they took in that view.

They took it all in.
And in their estimation
they found all of it,
their view over all of it,
the sum of all of it,
to be fair.

END OF PLAY

JACKIE SIBBLIES DRURY's plays include *Marys Seacole*; *Really*; *Social Creatures*; and *We Are Proud to Present a Presentation about the Herero of Namibia, Formerly Known as Southwest Africa, from the German Sudwestafrika, Between the Years 1884–1915*. Her work has been supported by Soho Rep., Theatre for a New Audience, LCT3, Berkeley Rep, New York City Players, Abrons Arts Center, Trinity Rep, Victory Gardens Theater, Bellagio Center, Sundance Theatre Lab, and The MacDowell Colony, among others. She has received many awards, including an Obie Award for *Marys Seacole*, a Windham-Campbell Literary Prize, The Susan Smith Blackburn Prize, and the Pulitzer Prize for Drama.

*Theatre Communications Group would like to offer
our special thanks to Jujamcyn Theaters
for its generous support of the publication of*
Fairview *by Jackie Sibblies Drury*

JUJAMCYN THEATERS (Jordan Roth, President) is recognized as a theatrical innovator, championing shows that push the boundaries of Broadway and create new experiences for audiences. The company owns and operates five Broadway theatres, including the St. James, Al Hirschfeld, August Wilson, Eugene O'Neill, and Walter Kerr.

TCG books sponsored by Jujamcyn Theaters include:

Fairview by Jackie Sibblies Drury
A Master Builder by Wallace Shawn
